They Found
a Common Language

Muslim mountaineers of one of Daghestan's many language groups listen avidly to youngster reading from a newspaper in their own local language.

They Found
a Common Language

Community through Bilingual Education

ILLUSTRATED WITH PHOTOGRAPHS

W. CAMERON TOWNSEND

1817

HARPER & ROW, PUBLISHERS
New York, Evanston, San Francisco, London

FIRST EDITION

LIBRARY OF CONGRESS CATALOG CARD NUMBER: 71-183630

Designed by Yvette A. Vogel

CONTENTS

FOREWORD

Linguists in Latin America and World Peace

On a recent visit to Colombia and Ecuador we saw firsthand
what the Summer Institute of Linguistics is doing and the tremendous value of its work. It is not only the scientific research,
far-reaching though it is, that is important, but also the humani-
tarian aspect of the work. Indian tribes that have been left
without the benefits of their countries' march of progress for
various reasons, generally injustice and lack of understanding,
are now being integrated. They, the original inhabitants, had
been forced, usually in the face of violence, to take refuge in
the deepest parts of the jungle or in mountain fastnesses, in
order to maintain their liberty, preserve their customs, and
save their lives.

Those are the places where the linguists of the Institute have
gone and we were greatly impressed by the working conditions
under which they labor. We found them living in a very austere
way right in the jungle villages, giving themselves without re-
serve to serving the Indian communities. We were also impressed by the efficiency and good coordination that prevailed

at the hinterland bases from which the Institute operates. The two-way radio service between jungle outposts and the base was adequate and vigilant. The pilots were capable and operate planes that are able to get in and out of difficult airstrips. The cattle program which is being promoted for the Indian communities is excellent.

All of these things identify the people of the Institute with the needs of mankind. They are free from selfish desires for financial gain as well as from all racial prejudices and discrimination. How we wish that this attitude prevailed everywhere so that humanity as a whole might benefit from the progress of science and creative capacity of men in peace. War among nations and strife between different groups of mankind would thus be eliminated through moral might.

CUAUHTEMOC CÁRDENAS

Mexico City
July 28, 1971

INTRODUCTION

Over fifty years ago I decided to leave my home in California to live among the Cakchiquel Indians in Guatemala, Central America. They intrigued me and were in need of help to integrate into the life of their fatherland. They were isolated from the mainstream of their nation by various formidable barriers that few of them had ever surmounted. One was the linguistic barrier. The men and some of the women could generally muster enough Spanish to buy and sell in the market places, but not many could speak it well. Their own language was Cakchiquel, a tongue so expressive in its verbal system that a single verb is conjugated in over 100,000 forms. Outside of their own homes and communities, however, most of the Cakchiquels were tongue-tied and hence considered inferior.

There were other barriers that also held them back. One was social. The ruling Spanish class would not even deign to shake hands with them. This was not due so much to race prejudice, for Indian blood had been blended extensively with that of the Spanish conquerors. It was a matter of social status.

The Indians were beasts of burden, ignorant objects of exploitation. Who wanted to mix with such? The laws at that time permitted a form of serfdom based on indebtedness. Most Cakchiquels were bound to coffee or sugar plantations by small interminable debts. These were fomented by drunkenness. If the Indian were about to pay off his debt, the landlord simply got him drunk and revived the debt with the cost of the liquor. Few of the Cakchiquels could either read or write, and if they could, the only books were in Spanish and who could understand sedate book Spanish? The consequent ignorance left them in the clutches of witchcraft and superstition that constituted still another formidable barrier. They were foreigners in their own fatherland.

After fifteen years in Guatemala, I founded the Summer Institute of Linguistics and began its activities in Mexico. I had been invited to work there by Professor Moisés Sáenz, one of the pioneers of the Indian education movement in that country. There, in some ways, the picture was much brighter. The Mexican Revolution had revolted against the idea that the Indians were inferior and had built a strong interest in giving them schools, land to farm, voting rights, and liberty to express their complaints *if* they could speak the language of government. There was the hitch. The rank and file could not. Much less could they read and write. They were masters of their own beautiful Aztec, but spoke a poor quality of Spanish if any at all. The ministry realized their need to learn the national tongue but was counting on the direct method and making poor progress. Then General Lázaro Cárdenas became President of Mexico (1934-1940), and he was sympathetic and helpful to the linguists and educators who wanted to try a bilingual approach. Bilingual education won out, but it is dependent on basic linguistic work and Mexico has 130 or more minority language groups. Therefore, the initial advance had to be among a few of the larger language groups only.

Convinced that Mexico was taking an important step that would be helpful to other lands, I transferred the scene of my personal activities to the jungles of Peru's great Amazon region. There in 1946, under contract with the Ministry of Education, my colleagues and I began linguistic research. The Indians were far more primitive than in either Guatemala or Mexico, and some were even savages. The Peruvian Government was right behind us, but its influence was not a daily or even a monthly occurrence along some of the rivers where our linguists had to live. Chiefs and witchdoctors exercised authority. Our intruding linguists had to depend on God's protection and a meek approach to chief and people through the local tongue as soon as that had been learned well enough to permit communication. Then late in 1952 the Minister of Education, at that time Gen. Juan Mendoza, decreed that Indians should be prepared to teach the Indians and in their own exotic tongues. Following this would come bilingual instruction (Indian-Spanish). As Indian teachers returned year after year from the training courses at Yarinacocha to their tribal habitats and taught men, women, and children to read in their own tongues, the word "savage" became obsolete. Even the word "primitive" headed on its way out as literacy spread and young products of the bilingual schools began going on to higher schools of learning and returning. Under the administration of Dr Francisco Miro Quesada as Minister of Education in the early sixties, the bilingual system was extended on an experimental scale to the millions of Quechua Indians of the highlands with excellent results. The project is expanding but the task is huge.

As our linguists of the Summer Institute of Linguistics entered into contracts with other multilanguage nations in different parts of the world for research and literacy, we came to realize more and more the gravity of language barriers. By the time we were working on 500 local tongues in 23 nations, we learned that there were 2,000 more to be studied. The

xii   THEY FOUND A COMMON LANGUAGE

progress of each of the 2,000 minority language groups that spoke them was blocked by the language barrier. Some efforts at least were being made in most countries to give all of their peoples a common tongue—the one that would make them truly full-fledged citizens of their native lands, but progress was *so* slow. In some countries the direct method was being used. Others were following the bilingual route that Mexico and Peru had taken. None had arrived . . . or so we thought until we learned that many minority language groups of the Caucasus had found a common language as a result of bilingual education. This book is the result of two fact-finding trips, in 1968 and 1969, to that part of the world. My hope is that it will be helpful to all lands where the problem of linguistic barriers exists.

I am greatly indebted to the Academy of Science of the Union of Soviet Socialist Republics and to the Academies of Science of each of the republics of the Caucasus, to educators, anthropologists, and linguists of Latin America and other parts of the world, several of whom are quoted verbatim in the text. As I extend my gratitude to them, I wish to include the friends who made our two visits to the Caucasus possible by their donations, as well as Dr. Esther Matteson and Mrs. Ann Eliza Tate who went themselves and interviewed many linguists and educators in Baku, Mahachkala, Tbilisi, and Yerevan for me. James Hefley, Shirley Heath, and Calvin Hibbard graciously helped me on the manuscript, and Dr. Heath further contributed important data, the fruit of her extensive research in preparing her book, *Telling Tongues: Language Policy in Mexico, Colony to Nation.** Then to the fine photographer that the Academy of Science secured for us, Leb Abramovich, goes my appreciation, and to Cornell Capa, a helpful friend of many years, who consented to edit the pictures.

* New York: Teachers College Press, 1972.

Most of all, I express gratitude to my dear wife Elaine who was with me in practically all the interviews, taking notes, making suggestions, winning friends, typing, encouraging, and before and after interviews spending countless hours studying the Russian language. An important part of her great contribution, however, goes back to her early utilization of local tongues in literacy work in the forties. I wish to thank my son Bill for his cooperation when he was only six years of age by learning rapidly to read English as I had written the lessons in my "Spanglish" orthography. He also rendered photographic help on our second trip to the Caucasus when he was nearly seventeen.

Finally, to my far-seeing friend of many years in Mexico, Cuauhtemoc Cárdenas, son of the great commoner, Lázaro Cárdenas, goes a big "thank you" for the clarity with which he sees the contribution that our linguists are making toward world peace.

W. CAMERON TOWNSEND

Waxhaw, North Carolina

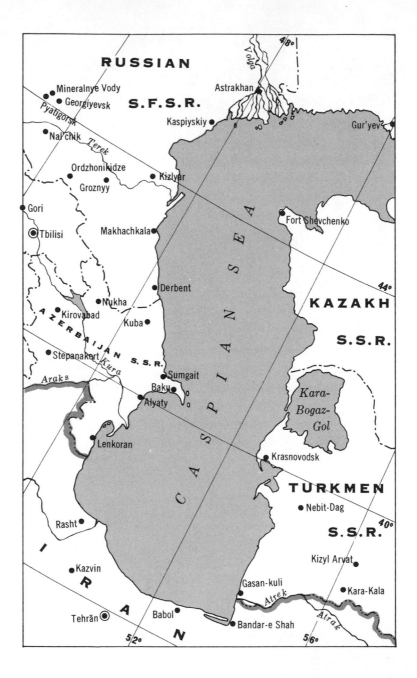

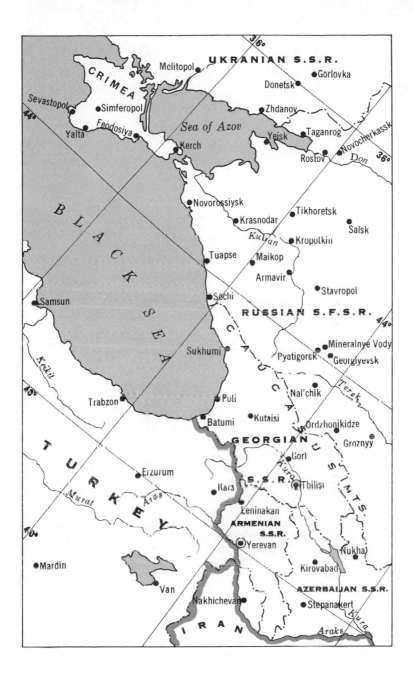

They Found
a Common Language

CHAPTER I

The Lesson of the Caucasus

It was no happenstance that Elaine and I were in Daghestan on the shores of the legendary Caspian Sea. The combination of circumstances that had taken us there went back over twenty-five years to before Elaine had become my wife. As a single girl she had joined the Summer Institute of Linguistics and was assigned to conduct literacy campaigns among various tribes of Indians in Mexico where our institute works under the Ministry of Education. Very soon villagers among the Aztec, Tzeltal, and Cuicatec tribes were reading in their own languages as a result of her efforts.

In 1946 Elaine had become my life partner and together we went to Peru. Our linguistic institute had contracted to give technical assistance to the Ministry of Education there in reducing the numerous Indian languages to writing and in teaching their speakers to read. The very first year we were in Peru, Elaine, an experienced schoolteacher, prepared primers and other literacy materials in the Aymara and Quechua languages of the highlands. Later she helped our linguists prepare

1

literacy materials for various language groups of the Amazon jungle.

Little did she or I realize at that time that some of the methods we and our linguists were using so successfully in giving alphabets to exotic tongues, combating illiteracy, and promoting bilingualism had been adopted far more extensively and with additional helpful features for over twenty years in the Caucasus and other parts of the Union of Soviet Socialist Republics. Nor were we aware of Lenin's strong regard for every man's mother tongue. We did know that when Christ's apostles began to proclaim the good news of redemption, every man heard in his own tongue wherein he had been born. We also knew that Lenin's followers had translated and published his writings in many languages of the U.S.S.R., some of them spoken by small ethnic groups. We did not know that bilingual education as it had been established by the new regime had completely transformed four republics in the Caucasus: Azerbaijan, Georgia, Armenia, and Daghestan. Moving as we did among linguists, we had heard something of the importance that the U.S.S.R. attached to linguistic research and the successes it had attained, but we were ignorant of the complete change of alphabets that had been accomplished in the Republics of Daghestan and Azerbaijan to facilitate unity, literacy, and education in general.

Years had passed. Linguistic research in tribal tongues, literacy, and, to some extent, bilingual education had spread to over 200 minority language groups in Latin America. Literacy crusades in the national languages (Spanish or Portuguese) had been organized in several countries, especially Mexico, Peru, and Brazil. One year Elaine had been called from our jungle headquarters in the Amazon forest to cooperate with Peruvian specialists in Lima in the preparation of literacy materials in Spanish for a nationwide campaign. They followed my psychophonemic method which speeds up learning to read

Schoolgirls in Baku, Azerbaijan. The necessity of bilingualism and additional language study does not rob these girls of their joy and does prepare them to meet the demands of a multilanguage society.

in a phonemically written language by its carefully worked out "piecemeal digestion of the alphabet." Then she was asked to lead the initial literacy campaign in a poor section of Lima at which university students were to be trained to hold similar campaigns all over the country.

It had been my privilege to attend some of the sessions. Scores of men and women for whom the printed page was mute came to learn night after night. I shall never forget their zeal and, on the part of one man especially, the tremor that accompanied his first approach to the light of the written word. He was a strong, energetic day laborer about fifty-five years of age. Unbelieving hope was written all over his sun-darkened features when Elaine encouraged him to think that he too could learn to read. Then she handed him the book. His hands trembled as he took it. Accustomed as they were to swinging the ax, the pick, and the shovel in caring for the parks of beautiful Lima, they shook with fear as the book brought him to the portal of a new day. A month later, however, someone reported that he had been seen in the park, reading with great satisfaction a newspaper that had been left on a bench.

The hope we had seen lighted in Peru, Mexico, Brazil, and other parts of Latin America was encouraging, but the insufficient number of torchbearers had limited its glow. Something more was desperately needed for both literacy and bilingual education. The reports that reached us from Asia, Africa, and the islands of the sea had told us of illiterate millions who could not even speak the national language of the countries where they lived. Then someone showed me the Bilingual Education Act of Congress, dated January 2, 1968, and through it we learned that in the United States of America there were "millions of children of limited English-speaking ability because they come from environments where the dominant language is other than English." The need of bilingual education on a large scale was evident in my own native land, and Congress had voted funds in this act "that additional efforts should be made to supplement present attempts to find adequate and constructive solutions to this unique and perplexing educational situation."

A French-Canadian friend in Peru, Bishop Gustavo Prevost, had told us of how he learned English as a second language. It was noticeable, however, that he was more eloquent in Spanish than in English. Yet he was Canadian and some of his

French-speaking Canadian priests did not even try to speak English. Obviously, if the U.S.A. were in need of bilingual education to unite her people, the two Canadas, English and French, would become truly one only as they also put forth more bilingual effort.

By that time we had learned that one great multilanguage area of the world stood out as having solved its former problem of wholesale illiteracy and linguistic divisiveness. That area was the U.S.S.R. The epitome of its success was the Caucasus. At the time we were in Mexico where, under the patronage of General Lázaro Cárdenas and his successors in the presidency, the work of our Summer Institute of Linguistics had grown to include the study of over one hundred Mexican Indian languages. With an indirect recommendation from General Cárdenas who was still living, we went to the embassy of the U.S.S.R. in Mexico City and told them that we wanted to visit the republics of the Caucasus and talk with their linguists and educators. We wanted to see and ponder for ourselves the great transformation that had been brought about. We wanted to learn the lesson of the Caucasus and pass it on to our lifelong friends in Latin America, to people who might listen in the U.S.A. and Canada, and to linguistic associates in many other parts of the world.

We knew that if nations in Africa learned the lesson and put it into practice they would have much more progress and far fewer intertribal tensions. Mexico, our adopted fatherland, with the experience it already acquired over the thirty years it had experimented with methods based on respect for each one of its 130 or more Indian tongues, was sure to listen. If it really went all the way, some three million "dialect"-speaking people who had been living for centuries as foreigners in their native land would be integrated completely into the mainstream of Mexico's national culture. Even India, with her many ancient cultures, might listen. How else could she unite her

Schoolboys with the author in Tbilisi, Georgia.

hundreds of language groups? And only with such unity could she become the power for progress that the natural gifts of her countless millions warranted for her.

The embassy in Mexico City had forwarded our request to the Academy of Science in Moscow, and so there we were on the shores of the largest and one of the most historic lakes in the world, commonly called the Caspian Sea.

CHAPTER II

Language-"Infested" Daghestan

The Caucasus is the most complex area in the Soviet Union, in national composition. . . . There are not many places in the world where a territory ten times smaller than France would be inhabited by several dozen nationalities.[*]

As we looked east across the Caspian Sea there was nothing visible but water, but we knew that along the far shore lay Central Asia with the Soviet Republics of Uzbekistan, Turkmenistan, and Kazakhstan.

We turned toward the west. In the foreground a park decorated the waterfront. Beyond it lay the railroad that had brought us from Baku and continued north toward where the Volga River emptied into the Caspian Sea. Then came the modest but extensive buildings of the city of Mahachkala. It was the capital of the Autonomous Socialist Republic of Daghestan. Such a republic is a subdivision within one of the

[*] *Moscow News*, Supplement to Issue No. 39 (1030), 1970.

7

The Linguistic Institute of the Academy of Science of Daghestan in Mahachkala, which has over 120 research workers.

English class in school in Baku. The textbooks are profusely illustrated, the teachers confident, and the pupils interested.

fifteen republics that form the U.S.S.R. but does have certain rights, giving it an autonomous status. Beyond our vision lay a narrow strip of former desert now transformed into irrigated vineyards and orchards, then foothills that we were to see later, and finally the high snowcapped mountains of the Caucasian Range that reached almost to the Black Sea. This jagged stretch of territory is the most language-"infested" area of the U.S.S.R. For educators faced with the problem of numerous languages within a given area the word "infested" is quite appropriate. To us with our linguistic bias, however, the exotic tongues in every valley and on each plateau intrigued like hidden treasure.

The legend is told that when an angel was sent to distribute a big bag full of languages all over the earth, he flew too close to a crag while over the Caucasus and ripped the bag. A hundred languages dropped out before he could close up the hole. He must have had plenty left, however, for today between four and five thousand mutually unintelligible tongues are spoken in the world. All are remarkable in structure, especially the ones spoken by groups of humanity that have had less contact with the outside world.

Eugene Nida, one of the world's most widely traveled linguists, wrote in a circular letter about a language group that he visited in Africa in the late sixties: "They are regarded by many as the world's most primitive people, but their language is one of the most delightfully complex and subtle, with incredibly complicated click sounds, four levels of tone, six common glides, and deceptively difficult diphthongs and triphthongs."

To the czars of Russia, however, and to many divergent rulers who had gone before them, the language barriers between one town and another of Daghestan were simply headaches. Each language group, however, was proud of its own form of speech, culture, and independence. A scholar of one

A street in Mahachkala. Most people live in apartment houses such as these. Parkways are consistently well cared for and the streets clean.

Homes in Daghestan rise on once-barren hills, thanks to new terraces and irrigation. This spot is between the shorelines of the Caspian Sea and the Dargin area. Close by on the north lies the Avar territory.

group told me of a former custom, illustrating their pride. If a special friend came to his friend's town but went to a hotel instead of to his friend's home, he would be killed in revenge by the insulted friend. The mountain people were fighters—fighting each other and also the invaders who varied over the centuries from Mongols to Tartars to Arabs to Turks to Persians and, last of all, to Russians under Peter the Great. Realizing the need of a common language, each of the conquerors, especially the Arabs, Turks, and Russians, sought to impose theirs. In Azerbaijan and Daghestan colonial powers succeeded, with the help of Muslim religious leaders, in making Arabic the official tongue but only so far as the scholars were concerned. The rank and file remained illiterate and clung to their own mother tongues. The czars had even less success, though Russian became the language of the courtrooms and executive offices.

Then came Lenin and the Revolution and a different approach to the old problem of multiple tongues. Fifty years later, out of the hodgepodge of one hundred tongues, has emerged one predominant and useful language. From one hundred strong proud wills has been forged one united people. Nevertheless, one hundred languages continue in daily use and one hundred wills find expression.

And after many years of personal experience in multi-language lands and a thorough acquaintance with the problems involved in such a transformation, we were anxious to learn more of how it had come about.

CHAPTER III

Revolution
from Gun to Pen

The peoples of Daghestan who formerly were the most backward in the Caucasus and who retained the most barbaric customs of the blood feud, who were constantly at war with one another over the mountain pastures and herds that had been stolen in ancient times, are now acquiring culture and are working peacefully together in the economic field.*

Daghestan has its own president, ministers of state, Soviet Council, University, and Academy of Science. Its president, we were told, was from the Avar language group, of which I shall have more to say later. Avars had been prominent in Daghestan affairs for over one hundred years. In the Mahachkala museum we saw a large painting, showing the surrender of the great Avar military leader of the nineteenth century, Shamil. He had held the czar's forces at bay for twenty-five years with Daghe-

---

* Nicolas Mikhailov, *Soviet Russia* (New York: Sheridan House, 1948), p. 111.

12

stanian fury and Muslim fervor but had finally been subdued.

The czars were able to subdue but not subjugate the Avars and the other fierce fighters of the many language groups of Daghestan. These simply drew back among their hills and mountains and let the Russians control the shoreline. But both the scholars and the leaders, whether in contact with the Russian rulers or not, spurned the Russian language and clung to Arabic. Those who wrote books or poetry did so in Arabic or, if they wrote in Avar, Dargin, Lezghian, or whatever local language was theirs, they used the Arabic alphabet. This alphabet, however, did not lend itself to writing languages in which vowels were more numerous and more important than in Arabic. Schools were very few and did not teach much more than the Koran. Very few men and almost no women knew how to read or write.

All this has changed. Today everyone reads. There are schools in all the towns and hamlets. The many nationalities esteem Russia as their benefactor and partner, and the Russian language is looked upon as the language of opportunity.

It was an Avarian scholar, the director of the Linguistic Institute of Daghestan, Gadji Danielov, who held us spellbound as he told about the surprising change of attitude toward the Russian language. He had sent his chauffeur to take us to his office at the Linguistic Institute where 120 specialists were at work under his leadership.

"In order to have a technical revolution," he said, vibrant with zeal, "you have to have a cultural revolution, and to have a cultural revolution you have to have a common language. The Russian language was as necessary as an electric light bulb is for light.

"There are eighty-seven languages and distinct dialects in Daghestan," he noted. "Many of them have been reduced to writing and are being used in the classroom. The first three grades are taught in the mother tongue. By this time the

Local headgear in a town of Armenia. This man belongs to one of the many language groups of the Caucasus.

average student has acquired something of a thirst for knowledge together with confidence in his ability to learn. Then the shift is made quite naturally to Russian. When the teacher explains that there are no more books in his language but that there are plenty in Russian, he says, 'All right, I'll learn Russian.' The radio stations here in Mahachkala broadcast programs in seven national languages as well as in Russian, but their use does not hinder the learning of Russian. Quite to the contrary, the very respect that is shown by all teachers to the local languages paves the way for the learning of Russian."

The cultural revolution that has come to formerly backward Daghestan with the help of a common tongue is also evident in the three Caucasian republics of ancient culture: Georgia, Armenia, and Azerbaijan. Customs, traditional attitudes, and family and social relations have all experienced radical change. Professor Danielov called it "revolution from a gun to a pen, from war to labor, from endless fighting to friendship." His heavy eyebrows fairly bristled as he said, "It's not just the fact that people can now read that's so important, but that they

A Lezghian citizen of Daghestan, wearing a typical turban.

can come to conclusions that bring about changes in every phase of life. Before, the mountain people had never heard of the United States of America or other distant places of the world. Now, not only do they know that these places exist but they also know much about each country."

My thoughts turned back to Latin America and transformations that had occurred among her aboriginal citizens. There was the Mexican Indian, Benito Júarez, one of the greatest statesmen that the Western Hemisphere has ever produced. He had spoken only the Zapotec dialect of Guelatao, Oaxaca, until when yet a child he moved to the city and was taken into the home of educated Mexicans. Then there was the son of a Ticuna witchdoctor at Cushillacocha on the Amazon River in Peru. He had learned quite a bit of Spanish at the Peruvian Government's bilingual school near his home, and then went to the Spanish-speaking city of Iquitos. There patriotic doctors took him into the General Hospital and trained him to be a practical doctor for his people. His witchdoctor father accepted his competition with pride.

I could think of others in many lands who had moved out of linguistic and cultural isolation into highly useful posts in the lifestream of their nations. Professor Danielov, however, was telling of wholesale transformation.

"How," I asked my host, "how did the transformation become so general? There must have been extraordinary cooperation between government officials, educators, and linguists. In the United States we spend a great deal of money on educational efforts among our local language groups such as the Navajos, but we are far from routing illiteracy and a big percentage have failed to master English, though the people are intelligent. How did the transformation of Daghestan become so complete?"

Professor' Danielov explained that talented boys and girls in large numbers had been selected in the 1920s and 1930s from among the local language groups and sent away to school in some educational center such as Kiev, Rostov, Moscow, or Leningrad. Some were sent as far away as Germany or France. In 1930 most of the Daghestanian students were sent to Rostov. He emphasized that it was absolutely essential for the area to have large numbers of teachers and engineers and they needed to be bilingual, in the local language and in Russian. Of course some had become linguists to prepare didactic materials. They began by working out an alphabet for each local language that required primers. The government provided ample stipends for all the students who were sent away to study. As an additional encouragement, the university entrance examinations that eliminated so many other applicants were waived for students from Daghestan.

With evident pride Professor Danielov assured me, "All the thousands of young folks who were selected from the local groups and sent off to study came back to serve their people. They didn't have to, but they did come back to help their nationalities. They had learned the Russian language, but they did not depreciate their own mother tongues. They had been taught that teaching must be done in the language of the local nationality."

Professor Danielov did not call the language groups "tribes," but rather "nationalities." His dark eyes shone at us from under those heavy eyebrows with the glint of a man who was well informed and confident.

He went on to state that those who returned to teach in the mountains or other rural areas were paid on the same basis as city teachers. Their schools were financed adequately. All those who returned to work as engineers in the building of roads, irrigation systems, and factories or as research workers under the Academy of Science or one of the institutes received remuneration comparable to that given to city workers. They also had opportunities to participate in politics. In local

The pomegranate counter in a section of the central farmers' market, Mahachkala, where various tongues are heard.

governments the prevailing voices were those of members of the local language group. Their language—as well as Russian—could be used in debate. They were sometimes sent to represent their local group in affairs of the union. The director of one of the linguistic institutes that we visited was a member of the Supreme Soviet in Moscow.

We went into the fruit and vegetable market in Mahachkala to see the farmers selling to the people of the city. Very definitely the people were an independent type. They were the kind that one would *ask* to do something but not *order*. The change that Professor Danielov told about had made them part of a larger whole without subjugating their inner souls to outside influences. True, the old unique styles of dress and the heavy veils for women had given way to a more European type of clothing. Trucks, buses, trains, and airplanes had replaced burros and the prancing steeds of yore. Tractors, ditchdigging machines, and other mechanized farming equipment that our chauffeur circumvented on the highways had replaced oxen-pulled plows. And, amazingly enough, there was unity instead of feuding among the local nationalities and with Russia, for whom they now had admiration and friendship. To us outsiders, they appeared friendly though reserved and very reticent about having their pictures taken. Their leaders, who spoke to us through our interpreter, expressed a real longing for international cooperation and peace.

CHAPTER IV

The Great Change
in Azerbaijan

On our second visit to Daghestan the interpreter that the
Academy of Science provided for us was a young lady of Russian background. Though she seemed to be completely identi-
fied with Daghestan, its people, and its new culture, we
naturally wondered if her background might not influence her
translations to us of conversations with Daghestanian linguists
and educators. Even Elaine, however, who knew more Russian
than I did, could not detect any Russian bias whatever on the
part of our interpreter. Evidently all local people had a local
outlook as far as the local horizon but were wholeheartedly
Russian in the outlook beyond.

In the Soviet Socialist Republic of Azerbaijan, just to the
south of Daghestan and still on the Caspian Sea, our interpreter
and guide, Professor Vagif Aslanov, was strictly Azerbaijanian
in appearance. His dark eyes, black mustache, and swarthy
complexion gave him the look of a scholar of completely Turkic
background on whom nothing of Russia had rubbed off except
the language. And he was indeed a scholar. He told us about

Azerbaijan's famous poet of the twelfth century, Nizami, the nineteenth-century poet and playwright, Mirza Fataly Akhundov, and other intellectuals of Azerbaijan's long literary history. He inspired us with his feeling for Azerbaijan's greatness. As we moved from institute to museum to market place to monument to the university to the Academy of Science to hotel, however, our guide often caused us to lose our own dignity by telling us, with great precision, clever jokes in English. He could also speak German, French, Arabic, and Persian. He cited changes in his own republic since it had been founded in 1921. We asked him about his background and learned that he was one of the results of that change.

Vagif Aslanov was born in the village of Poylie back in the mountains some 300 miles from the capital of Azerbaijan. His father and mother never learned to read and write, though they profited from their country's new day in other ways. Principally for them it was education for their two boys. One had remained in the village as a shepherd on a communal farm. His three daughters had finished their basic education in the village and then, as do many other young people from the villages, moved to Baku for higher training. One daughter had become a librarian and another a research worker in the Petroleum Institute, while the third is still studying at the University.

The status of women in Azerbaijan has changed completely. When Mexico's labor leader of some years past, Lombardo Toledano, had visited Baku he asked to meet the head of one of the large oil fields. To his great surprise the "boss man" was a young woman thoroughly trained in petroleum engineering. Lombardo Toledano reminisced when reporting the incident in Mexico that had she been born eight or ten years earlier, she might have been sold to a satrap for his harem. A booklet on Azerbaijan, published by Novosti Press Agency, Moscow, reports:

Factory for adding machines, etc. in Armenia. *Novosti Press Agency*

Apartment houses in a new area on the outskirts of Tbilisi.

Such ignominious survivals of the past as temporary marriages, the custom forbidding the bride to speak in the presence of her male in-laws, digging a woman's grave deeper than the grave of a man, regarding the birth of a daughter as a misfortune and buying a bride have been completely eliminated.

The Republic of Azerbaijan and the State of North Carolina are about equal in population, though North Carolina is about 50 percent larger in size. Azerbaijan, however, is more mountainous and though it is farther north by about four degrees latitude, it has a more varied climate. The Novosti Press booklet relates:

The climate is as varied as its relief map. While the sea at the windswept coast in the north is often frozen over, in the south, at Lenkoran, there is a realm of perennial green and humid subtropics . . . there are eight varieties of climate in the small territory of Azerbaijan.

The most important variation to us, however, was linguistic. Imagine newspapers at every stand in three different languages: Azerbaijani, Russian, and Armenian, and sometimes Georgian or Lezghian! Back in the mountains are found other languages such as Tatar and Lak, though they are very few in comparison with Daghestan. The differences, both linguistic and racial, are enough in two of the areas to call for the type of semiautonomous government that the U.S.S.R. provides in its policy of keeping each local group happy and cooperative in the overall program. It would be as though North Carolina set up an autonomous Cherokee Republic in the Cherokee part of the state for the 38,000 Cherokees to rule and an autonomous Afro-American Republic in the eastern lowlands where most officials would be black. In both, not only would English be the official language, but also Cherokee in the one case, and the local brand of Black English in the other.

Doubters who cannot believe that such government actually

The famous linguist, Professor A. C. Chicobava, lectures in his native Georgian language at the University of Tbilisi. Georgian script appears on the blackboard.

exists in the Caucasus should consult Nicolas Mikhailov's book, *Soviet Russia*. In referring to the Highland Karabakh Autonomous Region in the southwestern part of Azerbaijan the author says: "This is a separate autonomous unit set up in accordance with the Soviet principle of giving every nationality [language group] the fullest opportunity for developing its own culture and using its own language."*

Would such a policy work for the Cherokees and Blacks of North Carolina, or in minority language groups of Latin America, India, and other lands?

* P. 121.

CHAPTER V

Literacy's Two-Year Handicap Removed

Why had Lenin been so determined that everyone in the U.S.S.R. should learn to read? He himself gave the explanation when he said: "Without complete literacy . . . without teaching the people enough to enable them to use books . . . it would be impossible to attain our desired objective, socialism." Accordingly on the 26th of December, 1919, in the midst of civil war, he signed a decree "Concerning Measures to be Taken to do Away with Illiteracy." One of the top officials in the Ministry of Education to which the gigantic task was entrusted was the hard-working educator, Nadeshda Krupshaya, Lenin's wife. Such was the importance that the new-born Soviet Government attached to the task of teaching all to read.

If the task was to be difficult in Russia proper where over half of the long-neglected peasants and day laborers were illiterate, what would it be in the Caucasus with its great diversity of languages and higher percentages of illiteracy? The numerous local tongues of Daghestan and the mountains of Azerbaijan didn't even have alphabets except as the educated few in some of the regions had adapted the Arabic script to the local tongue. But even this was not common, for the "holy" language was Arabic itself and the scholars used it extensively. Apart from Russian, practically all the writing done in Daghestan and Azerbaijan and among the Turkic peoples of Central Asia was, as we have seen, in the Arabic script. Accordingly, that was the alphabet used in those areas in the feverish making of primers and textbooks for the great literacy campaign that was getting underway.

On our first visit to Baku it was our privilege to meet one of the patriarchs of the literacy movement, Salim Melim. He was present when we met with linguists and educators of the Academy of Science and also at our meeting with the rector and specialists of the university. His hair was gray and his face wrinkled, but his smile was captivating and his voice rang with enthusiasm and confidence. The other scholars in the conference room treated him with special respect. In fact, they used the venerable title "Melim" together with his name when referring to him. He was a veteran of the great campaign that had brought the light of literacy to his native Daghestan, and now he had relaxed to a less strenuous task at the Linguistic Institute in Baku.

We had some priceless opportunities to converse with Salim Melim, for he invited us to dine at his apartment and another time took us by car to his seaside *dacha* or summer home for recreation and a meal. Then he and his wife and little granddaughter accompanied us on the train trip from Baku to Mahachkala and stayed with us there for a few days. Everywhere he was treated as a living symbol of the change that had taken place. He had been among those who learned to read and write in Arabic script. Then he had been selected to study in Russia where he learned the language of Lenin. In 1928 he had welcomed the change from Arabic to the Latin script because it made his literacy work among the local language groups of Daghestan so much simpler.

The early thirties had seen Salim Melim coming and going

over the mountain trails visiting new schools, encouraging the recently trained teachers, and pointing the populace along the path of progress. He and his Russian- or Georgian-trained associates not only rode their Arabian mounts from village to village to visit the schools, but they also met with the teachers in conferences and institutes. The early teachers had learned to write in the old dot-bedecked strokes and twirls of Arabic script. If they had studied in Russia they had learned to use the Russian alphabet, and after 1928 they were teaching with Latin characters. Naturally they needed the help of experts.

As the drive for literacy continued more and more, Daghestanian and Azerbaijanian young people who had been sent away to educational centers in Russia to become engineers, teachers, or linguists would return. Through them, more and more favor built up for the Russian, or Cyrillic, system of writing.

An unsatisfactory alphabet is a great handicap to a people. As George Bernard Shaw pointed out continually, English is one of the worst. The alphabet has five vowels and all five are used at times to represent one sound.* One sound may be represented in twenty-one different ways. Numerous sounds are represented by the same letter or combination of letters. Learning to read is a matter of memory and takes time. Similarly, while the Arabic orthography continued to be used, children were taking two years in learning to read and it was even more difficult to teach them to write. Even high school students were often poor at writing in the alphabet of Mohammed.

When in 1928 the Republic of Turkey, with several times the population of Azerbaijan, gave up the Arabic way of writing and shifted to a Latin script, Azerbaijan and Daghestan did the same. Eleven years later all the twenty-two groups in the

---

* An example of how all five vowels may serve to represent one sound in English (based on pronunciation as found in *The Random House Dictionary*, 1967): forward—a = û; herd—e = û; bird—i = û; word—o = û; purr—u = û.

Lezghian schoolgirl in English classroom, Kasumkent.

U.S.S.R. that speak Turkic dialects and also the many language groups of Daghestan made a second change of alphabet, incredible though it seems. This time the Cyrillic alphabet was made standard so that a child who has learned to read Lezghian, Avar, Azerbaijani, or any of the local languages of the Caucasus (except Armenian and Georgian) can almost immediately read Russian. Today the first grader either has learned to read before he starts to school or else he learns in two or three months' time. Freed from the two-year handicap of difficult spelling and with the basis of unified writing laid for far-reaching linguistic unification, the new educational movement increased momentum.

Professor Aslanov told us that in his home town, Poylie, before the Revolution no one knew how to read. Today all of the 1,200 inhabitants who are seven years old and above are literate. The same holds true for the whole republic, for the most out-of-the-way town receives the same attention from the educational system that the cities do. Today about one-third of the population of Azerbaijan either is in school or is taking correspondence courses. There are 5,491 general education schools in the republic. Education is free and it is compulsory to go to school through the seventh grade. Many take advantage of opportunities for higher training. Before the Revolution there were only three technical schools in Azerbaijan. Today there are seventy-eight. At the beginning of the century there were only twelve engineers and twenty medical doctors of Azerbaijan nationality. Today there are over 15,000 doctors, and on the staffs of 118 scientific centers, there are 12,000 scientists. There were 133,000 college students in 1965.

Regarding education in the U.S.S.R. as a whole, the 1972 *World Almanac* states:

> *In 1968 there were 41,444,000 students in 8-year primary-polytechnical schools; 14,500,000 in secondary, evening and vocational schools and junior colleges; 4,300,000 in institutes of higher learning. Illiteracy was reduced to 1.5%.*

Now the twenty million people in the U.S.S.R. who speak one of the twenty-two Turkic languages use the Russian script in their publications and their writing. Each local tongue, of course, in forming its own alphabet, has to make certain modifications, as in the case of Azerbaijani, where six letters had to be added.

Twenty years after the Arabic script was abandoned, John Gunther was able to report that in Abkhazia, a small autonomous portion of the Soviet Socialist Republic of Georgia, everything possible was being done to promote the local Abkhazian culture and literature. Books were being published in the Abkhazian language. The Minister of Education of Abkhazia told him that 170 of the elementary schools in this local area are taught in Abkhazian, ninety in Georgian, eighty to ninety in Armenian, and seventy in Russian. Gunther further reported that in Tashkent in Central Asia, "schools exist for all the

* New York: Newspaper Enterprise Assn., Inc., p. 569.

recognized minorities. But a Kazakh boy going to a Kazakh school in Tashkent has to work hard: instruction is in his own language, but both Russian and Uzbek are compulsory as well."*

Bilingualism (Russian and local tongue) has spread far and wide. We noticed that the names of schools and universities always appeared on the buildings both in the local language and in Russian. Since the Autonomous Socialist Republic of Abkhazia is part of the Soviet Socialist Republic of Georgia and many Georgians live in its beautiful capital city, Sukhumi, traffic signs may be in their language as well as in Abkhazian and in Russian. Many Armenians live in Sukhumi also, and so we saw that language included in some of the traffic signs. The Armenian system of writing is different from Georgian script and both are different from the Russian alphabet which is used for Abkhazian. Four languages and three orthographies on one signpost convinced us completely of the recognition given to the local languages in the Caucasus. They are being paralleled with Russian but not substituted.

In Yerevan, the hustling, bustling capital of Armenia, we visited a school where most of the instruction is given in English by choice of the parents. But the youngsters also take some courses in Armenian and in Russian.

Just imagine hundreds of schools in Texas being taught in Spanish as well as in English, or many in Arizona being taught in Navajo, others in Oklahoma using the Cherokee tongue, and here and there other schools being taught in Swedish or Polish!

We should remember that this policy of the U.S.S.R. regarding the freedom of choice of language for schooling doubtless explains to a great extent both the absence of illiteracy and the goodwill that exists between peoples whose mother tongues are different. But basic to the progress in Daghestan and the Turkic areas was also the change of alphabet.

* *Inside Russia Today* (New York: Harper & Row, 1962), pp. 474, 498.

Tape recorder helps to give pupils and teachers a better pronunciation of English. The teaching of foreign languages begins early. Visual aids and good textbooks also help.

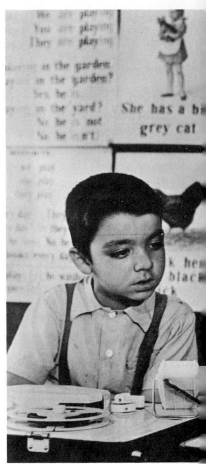

CHAPTER VI

A City
of Institutes and Petroleum

When we looked out of our hotel window across a park whose trees and shrubs betrayed a climate that was strangely tropical for Baku's latitude, we were freezing, due to an unusually cold winter as well as to inadequate heating facilities. We wondered how palm trees could stand the snow and ice. Baku is the fourth largest city of the Soviet Union situated on a beautiful bay of the Caspian Sea.

The air was pure and invigorating with no trace of petroleum odors though wells and refineries were not far away. Prior to the Revolution they had produced 90 percent of the oil used in the Russian empire and still produce 11 percent of what the U.S.S.R. consumes. Oil had been the main source of income for the region since the latter part of the nineteenth century, with fortunes being made by both Russian and foreign developers. Gasses, however, polluted the air, with travelers reporting "big thick cakes of soot falling on the town like big black snow." Today the city is clean and the air pure because, we were told, the whole technological process of refining the oil is vacuum sealed.

What interested us even more in this day of deep concern over ecology was the fact that there were 20,000 students in the local Petroleum Institute and that practically all of them were from Azerbaijan or some other part of the Caucasus. Our interpreter, Professor Aslanov, reminded us that he had a niece there.

The head of the Petroleum Institute was, at the time, also head of the Academy of Science of Azerbaijan of which we were guests. We visited its huge building high above the city and looking out over the Caspian Sea. The sight was majestic with beautiful Baku Bay stretched out below us. The building impressed us even more. How did the scientists of Azerbaijan rate to have a building like that? We had seen no commercial buildings anywhere in Moscow, Leningrad, or the Caucasus that began to compare. The government building down in the park by the shore was beautiful but not nearly so large. No military structures were to be seen except ancient relics like the Maiden's Tower, a symbol of many centuries of conquest or subjugation, whichever way you want to look at the coming, ruling, and going of Arabs, Mongols, Persians, and Turks.

The outstanding building of Baku's entire landscape, even outranking the main university building not far away, was indeed the Academy of Science. Across the street another building was being constructed for the academy's use also. It will house the Institutes of Physics, Chemistry, Mathematics, Cybernetics, and Oil Processing. The first and second floors of the main building held the library, and the top or ninth floor held a Museum of Science. In between were the Institutes of Economics, Philosophy, Literature, Linguistics, History, and Geography. Also there was the Institute of Peoples of the Middle and Near East and, some distance away, the Pedagogical Institute of Language. In the latter, 8,000 students pursued their courses. About thirty-seven other institutes were working on their specialties in the same city. Some were like colleges, but others had only research workers.

The main building of the Academy of Science of Azerbaijan in Baku.

We were taken to the fifth floor to the office of Academician Sheralev, director of the Linguistic Institute. He looked Turkish like most Azerbaijanians and was as businesslike as he was cordial. He told us that his institute employs over 150 research workers. Since our concern was in the field of descriptive linguistics as well as in alphabets and literacy, he called in the ones he thought we would find most helpful. The conversation was interesting and informative, though it did delay the consumption of the fabulous persimmons that were in the center of the table around which we sat. The local name of the delicious fruit sounded like "Persia." This reminded us that we were near the old Persian frontier, the part of old Persia now called Iran, where there are millions of people whose mother tongue is Azerbaijani.

Average research workers receive monthly salaries of about 320 rubles ($352 official exchange), more than a regular medi-

Capitol Building, Baku.

cal doctor gets. Everyone from bootblack to mayor seemed to be paid enough to live on but not much more, except possibly in the case of scientists. Few had automobiles, but since the city had good and very inexpensive surface and subway transportation, cars were not so essential. Taxis were rather plentiful and low priced. Most things of course belonged to the government.

The government needs scientists and seeks to encourage them, and so scientists, including linguists, are relatively better paid than others. Well-paid linguists and plenty of them! What a novelty! I thought. I had spent most of my life in multiple language countries where linguists were needed badly to pave the way for literacy workers, but where they were paid so little, few chose the career. In Darwin, Australia, I had visited the head of the Department of Welfare in the Northwest Territory where there are many difficult aboriginal languages. I asked him how many linguists he had in his employ and he replied, "I had *one* but lost him to the Government of New Guinea where there are seven hundred languages and not many linguists!" Most of the linguists I knew who actually lived among the peoples whose languages they studied were idealists who chose that career primarily to serve their fellow men.

The second time we were in Baku (October 1969) the university was looking forward to its fiftieth anniversary. The Soviet Socialist Republic of Azerbaijan had been formed on April 28, 1920, the university being founded just five months later. It is hard to understand how it could have been expected that there would be students for a university so soon, inasmuch as up until then, there had been very few schools. Those schools were conducted by someone who had taught little besides the reading and writing of Arabic passages from the Koran. The university nevertheless was started and during the next fifty years played a tremendous role in the life of the republic. Today every town and village in Azerbaijan has at least one school— some two or three. There are schools for the blind, deaf and dumb, and also for the retarded. Stiff entrance examinations prevent many young people from attending the university; still, when we were there 13,000 students were enrolled. In 1969 sixteen were attending from the village of Poylie. Each student receives a stipend to pay for his room, board, and recreation. Books also are provided by the government. Many who are not enrolled are taking correspondence courses.

As part of the preparation for the fiftieth anniversary celebration, the Linguistic Department of the university, together with the Institute of Linguistics of the Academy of Science, had organized a conference on the twenty-two Turkic languages of the U.S.S.R. Delegates had come from Central Asia and other regions of the Soviet Union where Turkic peoples live and continue to use their mother tongues. I asked our interpreter,

Professor Aslanov, if the languages were mutually unintelligible. He assured me that certain tongues have only brief periods of difficulty, and as an example compared a speaker of general American English who would not understand Cockney English too well the first few times he heard it with an Azerbaijanian visiting Turkey the first time, who would have a similar problem for a day or two. But other Turkic tongues such as Uzbek and Mongolian are very different one from the other.

Academician Sheralev invited us to visit the conference. He himself escorted us from the Academy of Science to the university auditorium where it was in session. As we entered, a Russian-appearing scholar from Central Asia was lecturing on the affixes of the language of Uzbek. He paused while Academician Sheralev introduced us and asked me to greet the assembly, which I did with pleasure. Then we listened and again were impressed to see how each man's language reigned. Each language merited careful study and analysis. Each was worth talking about and had elements that the native speaker could be proud of and professors could lecture and even brag about. Of course, in the background there was Russian, a very useful tongue employed by everyone who was ascending very far up the ladder of learning.

Things had changed in Baku. Once it had been a city of black gold—gold for outsiders—but for its own people, a city of ignorance and poverty. Now we found it to be a city of many institutes and halls of learning.

CHAPTER VII

Baku's Primary School Number 90

Our son Bill accompanied us with his camera on our second trip to the Caucasus. He found the Caspian Sea more intriguing than the institutes with their incomprehensible flow of Azerbaijani and Russian. But it seemed so *far* away. Far away, yes, from the hamburgers and malts that Bill longed for. Actually, however, the Caspian Sea has been near the center of historic happenings for almost three millenniums. Around this area of the world had moved Medes, Assyrians, Romans, Persians, Arabs, Mongolians, Turks, and, after 1804, Russians. All had come, all had seen wealth to win, and all had conquered for a period, though they had pillaged and destroyed as well. The czars had ruled for over a hundred years, bringing protection from the Turks and Persians, but also poverty and feudalism to the peasants.

The Caspian Sea is indeed interesting. It has no outlet, inasmuch as it is 85 feet below sea level. Its surface measures 169,-381 square miles. Its large sturgeon produce most of the caviar eaten in the world. Many different peoples, speaking different languages, live along its desertlike coasts where irrigation is necessary to produce crops. There they also dig underground or underwater to get oil. The four republics that surround it on the west, north, and east are members of the Soviet Union. But on the south lies Iran, where, we were told, the millions of Azerbaijanians who live there continue to write in Arabic script and wear distinctive garbs, including the heavy veils for the women.

Regarding the Turkic people on the eastern side of the Caspian Sea called Uzbeks, I was interested to read somewhere the following:

> To detail the massive character of the Soviet educational effort in Central Asia, the Uzbek Republic . . . provides an apt illustration. Before the Revolution only 2% of the population was literate. There were no native engineers, doctors, or teachers with a higher education. In short, Central Asia was no different in this respect from most of the colonial dependencies of the European powers, and worse off than many
>
> Today, in the Uzbek Republic alone, there are 32 institutions of higher learning, more than 100 technicums, 50 special technical schools, 12 teachers' colleges, and 1,400 kindergartens. Nearly 2,500,000 children attend school, and more than 50% of its teachers have had some higher education. In addition, the Republic has an Academy of Sciences and an Academy of Agricultural Sciences. The rate of literacy is over 95%. The Republic before the Revolution possessed no public libraries; today there are nearly 5,000. The number of books printed in the Uzbek language in 1913 was 118,000; today it approaches 19 million. When this record is compared with that of Iran, Afghanistan, the Arab countries, the states of Southeast Asia, or even Turkey, all of which were at a comparable or more advanced level of educational attainment in 1914, the achievement is impressive.

Whether in a city like Baku, therefore, or on the eastern shores of the Caspian Sea or a communal farm back in the mountains of Georgia, the same thirst for knowledge existed. Laurens van der Post wrote in his book, *A View of All the Russians,** after visiting a collective farm:

> *We passed the single room that served as a farm school. It was full of children who looked not as if they were taking instruction, but listening to a fairy tale. This enchantment with education of people, children, teachers and leaders everywhere runs like a thread of gold through my impressions of the Soviet Union.*

Elaine and I observed this attitude on the part of the children in Baku's Primary School Number 90. The director of the Foreign Department of the Academy of Science, Professor Shamil, took us there. He was an amiable young man with pronounced Azerbaijanian or Turkish features. As we rode along the clean, orderly streets of Baku in the car he had brought for us, I told him of some of the problems my wife and I were having with the Russian language of which he seemed to be a perfect master. Finally, I said in Russian, so as not to bother our interpreter, and since it was one thing that I could say, "If I didn't believe that God would help me, I would give up the study of the Russian language." He replied, "I'm an atheist and I speak four languages." I smiled and said, "Yes, and if God were helping you, you would probably speak twenty." We had a good laugh and then we were at the large school in the heart of the city.

The principal was a woman. She and a few of the teachers, both men and women, gathered to greet us and show us around as soon as Professor Shamil explained the purpose of our visit. We first went to an English class and then to one in Persian. In the latter a girl with Turkish features and about thirteen years old was reciting. Her own language was Azerbaijani and of

---

* New York: William Morrow & Co., 1964, p. 122.

Primary School Number 90, Baku. The name and certain information about the school appear in Azerbaijani on the reader's left, and in Russian on the right. Standing with Dr. and Mrs. Townsend are the director, two teachers and several pupils, as well as the representative of the Academy of Science.

course she spoke Russian well. She doubtless heard the first at home and the second in the homes of some of her friends. She would hear both at school, on the street, and over the radio, but she had very little contact with Persian. Nevertheless, she seemed to know it quite well. I asked her to write the word for Friday in Arabic script. She did so with perfect ease and what a jumble of dots and lines it seemed to me! It consists

A girl in Primary School Number 90, Baku, recites in Persian class. She is bilingual in Azerbaijani and Russian.

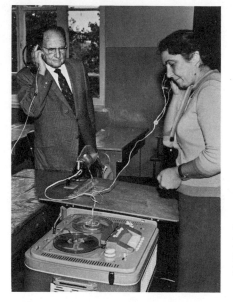

The author listens to English lesson on tape in Primary School Number 90, Baku.

of about twelve jagged twirls of the chalk in a row, sprinkled above and below with twelve dots that had to be located just right.*

I suppose that that word is the most striking example of the difficulties of Arabic script. I hope so. A story has come down from a century ago that would seem to indicate that it is at least one of the worst. The renowned Mirza Fataly Akhundov arrived late for a dinner engagement. He was asked the reason for his tardiness and he replied, "At the last minute I had to write the word Friday, and it took me so long to write in the dots above and below that it made me late."

The teacher of Persian showed us the linguistic laboratory which included tape recorders and playback equipment. We also found the equipment in the chemistry and physics laboratories to be quite impressive to us whose knowledge of those subjects was sadly lacking.

It was the noon recess when we said good-bye and so a few of the youngsters, as well as the principal and some teachers, stood with us in front of the main building when the Russian photographer who accompanied us took our picture. I have studied that photograph time and again. The studious expression and neat, intelligent appearance of the pupil who had recited in Persian seemed to be typical of the oncoming generation of Azerbaijanians preparing to meet their southerly neighbors when they come on business, pleasure, or sport. The stern firm features of the principal are another object of study. She had held her position for twenty-four years. Her Moslem mother doubtless would have feared the men that her daughter, as principal, routinely directs. Her face tells of victory through struggle. It represents the new day for women in all the Moslem, or at least formerly Moslem, regions of the U.S.S.R.

Baku is an international city, a sort of melting pot of nation-

---

* The Azerbaijanian word for Friday in Arabic script: ﺑﻴﺸﻨﺒﻪ

alities. The people mix without regard to race. There are no ghettos. Visitors come as tourists, artists, and/or to attend conferences. In 1964 the Second Afro-Asian Solidarity Conference was held in Baku with representatives in attendance from several countries on those continents. We were given hotel rooms on the condition that we would leave one day earlier than planned because all rooms had been reserved for delegates from far and wide to a conference on petroleum.

CHAPTER VIII

Downtown Grapevines

We came to appreciate our interpreter. Professor Vagif Aslanov knew just where to take us. He never hurried us whether we were buying Italian-made shoes at a low price in the dollar store or asking questions of linguists and teachers or looking at treasures of art and literature in the museums. He spent a great deal of his time with us and that without remuneration. Not only scholars but also laborers gave us the impression that money was the last thing that interested them. We have never visited or lived in any other country where money seemed to play such an insignificant role in people's thinking.

I recall our visit to the capital of Armenia. My watch needed repair. Our guide, Professor Vahe Aftandilian, was an outstanding linguist and founder of the Yerevan English School. He was also professor of English, French, and Persian at the university. He took us to a repairshop on the main thoroughfare. When I picked up the watch later, I asked for the bill. There was no charge! Also in Yerevan I had to see a dentist. Again no bill after two hours of expert work! On our first visit to the

Caucasus when the weather was so unusually cold, we had to receive medical attention for coughs and congestion. Some of the treatments seemed strange to us, but stranger still, they were all free.

Vagif Aslanov really made us feel at home in Baku. Having grown up in a village back in the mountains, there was something plain and unsophisticated about him that appealed to us strongly, and yet his mind was so keen, his mustache-trimmed face so dignified, and his eyes so dark and deep, we would have been just a bit nervous in his presence but for the very evident warmth of his friendship. How he could take care of his classes and us and still be so carefree was remarkable, and we appreciated it greatly.

He gave us examples of the three systems of writing that had been used in Azerbaijan and Daghestan during his lifetime. The first of the three, Arabic script, had been on its way out when he was born, but his examples of it were the most intriguing. For instance, he wrote in Arabic script the words for *love* ﺣـﺐ , *eye* ﺳـﯿﻦ , and *word* ﺳـﻮﺭ , and then showed how by taking off a dot, *word* was changed to *salty* ﺳـﻮﺭ and *eye* was changed to *blind* ﻛـﻮﺭ , and by moving one dot from below to above the word, *love* became *distress* ﺣـﺐ . He took us to a concert where we heard Azerbaijanian musical wailing done by a soloist whose baritone voice and breath endurance were exceptional! My dear wife, with keen appreciation of voice, called it fantastic music; I called it wailing.

At the market place we bought fruit and enjoyed watching the people from the countryside. It was across from the main subway station. Baku does go underground for more than oil. It now has subway trains for rapid and inexpensive transit. Moscow has been proud for years of its superb subway that transports over two million people a day for about five cents a ride. Now Baku has its fine subway.

Near the center of the city is a monument erected to the memory of the twenty-six Bolshevik commissars who had been executed in 1918, when counterrevolutionary forces overcame the Bolsheviks who had been in control for nine months. I was only casually concerned with the political side of things, but there was an aspect of this monument that did interest me. Stephan Shaumyan, president of the Baku Council of Peoples' Commissars and one of the twenty-six heroes who had met their death, was the father of one of today's great linguistic theoreticians of the U.S.S.R. and of the world, our personal friend, Professor Stephan Shaumyan.

Though linguistics and bilingual education played a very important part in the progress of the Caucasus, I realize that these two forerunners of progress and unity in a multilanguage situation cannot succeed by themselves. Behind them there has to be a government that places education and the cultural progress of people of any and every tongue first and foremost in its program. It must be willing to spend the money necessary to carry on year after year. The results would indicate that that type of government must have existed most of the time in the four republics of the Caucasus during the past fifty years.

We had very little contact with officialdom in the U.S.S.R., none actually aside from the mayor of one city and an official in the Ministry of Education in another. State or city officials in person or by portrait were seldom seen wherever we visited. We seldom saw anything that savored of political propaganda except the references to labor and legendary Lenin. Those were everywhere! We were impressed by the scarcity of policemen and traffic cops. The people always seemed to take law and order as a matter of course. We concluded that one important explanation of the remarkable success in education as well as the incredible care of some downtown grapevines we saw was the attitude of the people themselves.

Grapevines climb the front wall of apartment house along a thoroughfare in Tbilisi.

Grapevines downtown? Yes. Baku and Tbilisi, the capital of Georgia, are large cities but hardy grapevines reach from the cement sidewalks to upper stories, providing fruit and shade for the apartment dwellers upstairs and beautiful greenery for the multitudes that throng the streets. I never had seen anything like it. None of the passersby plucked a leaf or damaged the vine. The vines had just enough protection to ward off accidental trouble, and no intentional trouble existed. In a sense, the vines belonged to the people who benefited from their fruit, shade, and frondage, but *everyone* took care of them. Granted that such cooperativeness has had a great deal to do with the success of bilingual education and alphabet reform, at the same time I must insist on the basic value of the methodology. In fact, I believe that when the methods are adequately fruitful the spirit of the people will be buoyed up and brought to the place where they will safeguard or, at least, not infringe upon that which brings help and joy to others.

Time and again as we encountered high moral standards and fine ethical attitudes in the U.S.S.R. we were reminded of the Bible. Unselfishness, neighborly love, respect for the rights of others, honesty, discipline, morality, and virtues so important in the formation of biblical character surrounded us to a remarkable degree wherever we went. Evidently the same biblical characteristics are stressed in China. In a striking editorial by James Reston of the *New York Times* (July 1971) entitled "Chinese Follow Moral Maxims the West has Forgot," he refers to the Chinese Communist doctrine and states that "the similarities with the dogmatism of the protestant ethic are not only unmistakable but unavoidable." Mr. Reston also refers to McGuffey Reader moral maxims as being kept before the Chinese people.

We found just that type of standards neatly printed on the wall of the hallway opposite the English classroom in a large school in Tbilisi. Twenty-one rules of conduct were listed, and they did sound as though they had been taken either from an old McGuffey Reader or based on Bible principles. They were in English for those pupils of English who met there daily, and were as follows:

REGULATIONS FOR SCHOOLCHILDREN
(Every pupil is obliged to keep these rules)

1. *Do your best in your studies.*
2. *Don't be late to the classes.*
3. *Come to school clean, well brushed and neatly dressed.*
4. *Keep your desk clean and tidy.*
5. *Take care of school property.*
6. *Never forget to bring to school all the necessary things/text-books, writing materials and other things/*
7. *Don't be noisy and don't run in the school.*
8. *Follow the pupil's daily routine.*
9. *Be attentive at the lessons.*

10. *Accurately enter all the home-tasks into your day-book.*
11. *Be well-disciplined and well-behaved.*
12. *Take an active part in your work.*
13. *Guard as your own the honour of your school and your class.*
14. *Help your parents with the house-work.*
15. *Obey your parents.*
16. *Take care of your younger brothers and sisters.*
17. *Be modest and polite.*
18. *Be obliging to the grown-up people.*
19. *Mind the rules of street traffic.*
20. *Always make way and offer your seat to old people and small children.*
21. *Keep your room clean; keep your bed, clothes and footwear in order.*

One time it was our privilege to entertain a young Russian diplomat and lawyer and his family at our home in North Carolina. Since it is our custom to read some portion from the Bible each morning after breakfast, I asked him to read for us the 13th chapter of First Corinthians. He did so and then said, "This sounds like one of the passages in our Communist Code."

The Summer Institute of Linguistics, which it was my privilege to lead until recently in its efforts on behalf of literacy, language unification, and progress among local language groups in twenty-three countries, works under contract with governments. Most governments will not tolerate sectarianism or religious fanaticism. Hence we are careful to avoid these while encouraging moral and spiritual uplift through portions of the Bible translated into the local tongues. Our experience corroborates what we saw in the school at Tbilisi and the lesson of the grapevines there and in Baku: a strong moral fiber in the people is basic to success in transforming groups through literacy and bilingual education. Many times I have seen the latter fail through dishonesty, immorality, drunkenness, and

Regulations For Schoolchildren

(Every pupil is obliged to keep the following rules)

. Do your best in your studies
. Don't be late to the classes
. Come to school clean well brushed and neatly dressed
. Keep your desk clean and tidy
. Take care of school property
. Never forget to bring to school all the necessary things (text-books, writing materials and other things)
. Don't be noisy and don't run in the school.
. Follow the pupil's daily routine.
. Be attentive at the lessons
. Accurately enter all the home-tasks into your day-book
. Be well-disciplined and well behaved.
. Take an active part in your work.
. Guard as your own the honour of your school and your class.
. Help your parents in the house-work.
. Obey your parents
. Take care of your younger brothers and sisters.
. Be modest and polite
. Be obliging to the grown-up people.
. Mind the rules of street traffic.
. Always make way and offer your seat to old people and small children.
. Keep your room clean; keep your bed, clothes and footwear in order

The principal of a large school in Tbilisi stands proudly beside the 21 rules of conduct.

strife. The great success attained in Peru by the government's bilingual schools among Indian tribes of the jungle has been due to the fact that early in the project a wise Director of Rural Education wrote a decree and secured the President of the Republic's signature. The decree stipulated that in the bilingual schools of the jungle instruction of a spiritual nature shall be given, utilizing the Scriptures of the Four Gospels, and of the New Testament. The results were quickly seen not only from the command to love one's neighbor instead of throwing a spear at him, but also from the terse instruction: "Speak every man truth with his neighbor."

A year or so later some of the Amuesha tribesmen were traveling downstream on a raft. They were on their way from their remote habitat to Yarinacocha where the government's training course for bilingual Indian teachers was held each summer. Indians selected from other areas and speaking other languages were also traveling toward Yarinacocha by boat, raft, or airplane. There were practically no roads nor even trails. The transition from log canoes to airplanes was made by primitive tribesmen in one leap, for they never had ponies, oxcarts, trucks, or buses. You either traverse the vast Amazon forest by river or fly over it by airplane, or stay put. A few of the tribesmen who had been selected to train for teaching lived where airplanes landed at times, but the majority, often from hundreds of miles north, south, or southwest, used a riverboat or raft.

The Amueshas were coming down the Pachitea River on a raft—a trip of two weeks' duration. Naturally some had brought their wives to do the cooking en route as well as to get some schooling at Yarinacocha. One gave birth to a baby right on the raft a week before they reached their destination. Her husband had done well enough in the previous year's course to receive his commission as a bilingual teacher (Amuesha-Spanish). At the course he learned that newborn babies had to be registered. Babies born in Amuesha country did not get registered because there were no government offices. Yarinacocha, however, was near the city of Pucallpa and so the proud school-teacher-father went there to comply with the law. To his consternation, however, the town clerk informed him that he should have registered the child within two days after birth. His baby was nine days old and still unregistered; he would therefore have to pay a fine of about five dollars. The father objected, saying that they had been several days' journey upriver where there was no way to register the child. The clerk replied that the law did not make any provision for such a contingency. Out of sympathy for him, however, she suggested that he swear that the child was only two days old and thus avoid the fine. The father bowed his head in thought. The year before he had been taught in the Amuesha language and in Spanish: "Speak every man truth with his neighbor," and now this woman was suggesting that he lie about the date of his baby's birth and save five dollars. He raised his head, looked at the clerk with utmost respect, and said, "Thank you, ma'am, but I'll pay the fine."

In this chapter we have moved from the Caucasus to North Carolina, to China, to the Amazon forest. We have pondered old-fashioned rules on the hallway wall of a progressive school in the SSR of Georgia. An outstanding editor has told us of McGuffey reader principles at work in China. We have seen the effect of the Bible's emphasis on love and honesty among once primitive Indians in Amazonia. One thing must be clear. There is a moral facet to the problem in hand that demands and facilitates the integration of the hosts of human beings now in cultural isolation. Some anthropologists say that we should leave them alone. These anthropologists talk about the "happy savage." After Arnold Toynbee had visited the Jungle Base of the Summer Institute of Linguistics of Peru, however, he said that the work of the linguists and teachers was saving the minority language groups of the jungle from falling victim to the juggernaut of progress. He was right for the area he had in mind and for vast areas elsewhere. In some areas society in general, for its own security, needs the proper integration of linguistically and culturally isolated groups. The solution has been demonstrated. It will work anywhere regardless of political ideology provided there is adequate concern, determination, and cooperation.

CHAPTER IX

We Visit
a Lezghian School

Daghestan holds several records. It not only has more local languages than any other region of the U.S.S.R., but it also has a higher percentage of centenarians and a higher number of children per family. In fact, we were told that whereas the number of children per family in Moscow is only 1.5 and a grave concern to officials there, in Daghestan a family generally has four or five children. Back in the mountains the average is higher and in the cities somewhat lower.

Through arrangements made by the Academy of Science we visited two areas back in the foothills where various local language groups are found. We had thought that we would be leaving the beaten trail, but the road to each language group was paved all the way. On each jaunt we went through several fair-sized towns. One, in fact, was a small city and an ancient one at that. It was Derbent, quite a distance due south of Mahachkala, the capital. We did not take time really to inspect the high walls and stone-paved inner halls and patios of its medieval fortress, but we were quite interested in what we did see.

From Derbent our route lay west as we left the seacoast and penetrated the foothills. From Mahachkala to Derbent the highway had traversed many vineyards, but as we left the sea and began to climb, the road became lined with fruit orchards. There were more apricots than any other fruit, which made me wonder if they had anything to do with the longevity of the people, as is said to be the case with a tribe in the Himalayas. At any rate, we met and talked with a Lezghian man whose age was given as one hundred and ten years, and we heard that there were at least one hundred couples in the mountains who had celebrated their one hundredth wedding

Longevity in the Caucasus: the old man in the picture is Shirali Muslimov, who lives in a village of Azerbaijan and is reported to be 162 years of age. *Novosti Press Agency*

Lezghian schoolteacher (center) in Tasumkent poses, during feast for his special guests Dr. and Mrs. Townsend, with the principal of the Lezghian school (second from right) and the Townsends' guide (extreme right), who speaks two local languages besides Russian. The two chauffeurs for the trip are the men with mustaches.

anniversary. I told my hosts that seventy-five more years with my Elaine would be so wonderful that I would like to move to their area and see what it could do for me. It seems, though, that only Moscow can give permission to a foreigner to live anywhere in the U.S.S.R. Autonomous republics such as Daghestan have autonomy in most local matters, and full-fledged Soviet Socialist Republics such as Azerbaijan, Armenia, and Georgia are said to have jurisdiction over all local affairs as well as a voice through their representatives in the overall affairs of the Soviet Union, but only the latter handles foreign affairs.

It might be a good idea to establish a Caucasian Longevity Colony for foreigners somewhere in the foothills of Daghestan. Kasumkent, where we went on this trip, would be ideal.

There, senior citizens, in quest of longevity, would be surrounded by tranquil hills, friendly Lezghians, apricot orchards, and the inspiration of high snowcapped mountains far off to the west. They probably would not want to stay very long, since they would be unable to speak with many of their neighbors, but even a few weeks might help.

Our party filled a small car and a Russian jeep. A linguistic student who spoke two tribal languages in addition to Russian was our official guide. He and our interpreter, Gala, rode in the car with Elaine and me. Leb, our Russian photographer, rode in the jeep, as well as our son Bill who took pictures in color. One of the two chauffeurs was an Avar.

We stopped at a country tearoom along the way where several travelers were taking refreshments. While we waited to be served we watched some Lezghian men eating pomegranates. Perhaps they noticed our eyes bulging at the sight of such large, colorful fruit, for what should they do but come over to our table with big smiles and offer us some. This friendly manner toward us was evident not only in the Caucasus but also in the restaurants of Moscow.

We arrived at Kasumkent at about nine o'clock at night. The teacher at whose home we were to stay, Tagir Shihzaguirabu, had not expected us until the next day, but he opened his home to us gladly. His wife Perizat immediately began cooking food for our entire party, which had grown with the addition of other teachers who joined us at a previous stop in Kasumkent until we numbered twelve. By midnight we were feasting on roast lamb, noodles with garlic and tomato sauce, fruit, and Lezghian bread. The home was new and large, twice as big probably as a teacher's home in Moscow. Even topnotch scientists in Moscow have relatively small apartments due to the overloaded building program and the surprisingly close, though not absolute, adherence to the policy of equality

Entrance to the Lezghian school, Tasumkent. Several of the teachers, together with the principal (right of Dr. Townsend and wearing necktie) and a few girl pupils, gathered around the Townsends for the picture. All the teachers are bilingual or trilingual. The women teachers wear scarves over their heads instead of the old Moslem veils that their mothers used.

whether the apartment dweller is a carpenter, storekeeper, or brilliant chemist.

In the Lezghian town we were visiting, however, it seemed that building materials were available, and if the teacher could do his own building or get his neighbors to help him, he was free to construct more ample living quarters. Professor and Mrs. Shihzaguirabu had doubtless received help from neighbors, for their home was two stories high with three large rooms above and below and large porches on each level. There were four large fireplaces. At one, Mrs. Shihzaguirabu had a white tile stove for cooking. There was no indoor plumbing or running water, although water was piped to the street corner and presumably would be brought into the house later. The three teenage Shihzaguirabu boys must have bunked on the floor, for we were given their room.

In the morning we went to see the large school where the boys were receiving a bilingual education and where their father was teaching. My wife, with her schoolteaching background, marveled whenever she visited the first grade whether the school was in the Caucasus or in Moscow. She found it hard to believe what she saw each time: first graders doing their arithmetic problems with pen and *ink* and not erasing. The lessons in their notebooks were neatly written. The same was true at the Lezghian school in Kasumkent.

The first three grades are taught in the Lezghian language. From then on the language of the classroom is Russian, though, in the fifth grade, the pupils are introduced to some foreign language. At least one hour of classes in Lezghian is continued through the ninth grade.

The classrooms have ample space and light. We walked along the large playground, but our visit was not at the right time of day for us to see any games.

The principal of the school had been selected as a lad to go off for training in Russia and had mastered the Russian language as well as the subjects he was going to teach. A neighbor of Shihzaguirabu's also seemed to be an able teacher, though we may have been prejudiced a bit by the fact that he and his wife had earlier brought us a jar of very delicious honey.

At the end of our visit to the school we were presented with textbooks in the Lezghian language and a Lezghian newspaper.

On the return trip to Mahachkala our big stalwart chauffeur turned on the radio, and we heard a broadcast in the Lezghian language. The only one in our party who could understand it was Kim, the guide from the Academy of Science, whose home

town was near the Lezghian region and belonged to the Taba-
saran group. Our chauffeur enjoyed listening to programs that
were broadcast in his language, Avar, but our interpreter,
Gala, preferred Russian. Programs were on the air in three or
four more local languages, we were told.

In Moscow we had been warned not to pick up the accent
with which the Russian language is spoken in the Caucasus.
At our stage of learning Russian the warning was highly com-
plimentary, but it made me think. We had heard our hostesses,
Mme. Salim and Mme. Danielov, conversing together with
animation. What language were they using? It must have been
Russian, for it is not likely that they hailed from the same
local language group. Certainly Professor Danielov at the conference at the institute had not greeted Professor Murkelinsky
in Lak nor had the latter greeted him in his beloved Avar.
They had used the common tongue, Russian, probably with an
accent and quite possibly without the difficult grammatical
finesse that one would hear from authors of dictionaries and
directors of institutes in Moscow and in Leningrad.

My thoughts leaped over the nine- or ten-hour difference
in time zones to the Puerto Rican Spanish-speaking section of
New York City, to parts of Texas, New Mexico, Arizona, and
California where Mexican Americans also cling to Spanish,
and to our new home in North Carolina where we had had
our first real introduction to Black English. For children in
those areas there was hope that through integration and other
efforts they would learn eventually to master English, but what
could be done for their parents? Elaine and I had attended
Sunday services at Black churches and had come to love the
Black people. When we decided to become members of one
of their churches, however, we did not choose one where the
form of spoken English was hard for us to follow, but rather
one where the pastor preaches in standard English, and where
the singing is almost what we are used to. Most of the members

of the church, however, vary enough from standard English that a white stranger, upon hearing one of them speak over the telephone, would immediately be aware that the speaker was a Black American. It would be very helpful if adult Blacks wherever Black English is used were given an opportunity to master standard English. It would be a valuable cultural reinforcement of theoretical equality. This does not mean the eradication of Black English any more than the teaching of correct Russian to an Avar aims at the eradication of the Avar language. One simply duplicates the other. People in the U.S.A. quite generally fail to realize that Black English is a language, but an investigator of Black English, Olivia Mellon, states: "Linguists who have studied the vocabulary and syntax of Black English find it to be a separate but equally valid language system with a highly developed structure of its own."*

In order, however, to duplicate Spanish, Black English, or any other language spoken in certain areas of the U.S.A., thousands of classes should be established for adults wherever progress of the people is hindered by what might be called their "differing lingo background." Lessons in English grammar and pronunciation could be given by trained volunteers.** In approach, these classes would be similar to what we had heard on the correct use of Russian at the Lezghian and Dargin

* Quoted from an article entitled "Black-English—Why Try to Eradicate It?" *The New Republic*, Nov. 28, 1970, p. 16.

** According to an article that appeared in *The New York Times* Nov. 14, 1971, a drive is underway to prepare volunteers to teach the functionally illiterate of various types and ages.

In a report by Dr. Donald G. Emery, Executive Director of the National Reading Center, operating agency of the National Reading Council, "the Center's goal . . . is to have 200,000 trained reading tutors in 20 states serving in communities and schools by the fall of 1972. . . . The National Reading Center will bring together 100 people from across a state in a two-day workshop. These 'tutor trainees' will return to their own communities and train 100 volunteers to be reading tutors, using materials developed by the Center. The tutors will teach the students."

schools. Divergent ways of speaking the national language that brand the speaker as different if not inferior would be done away with, and adults as well as children of the areas of the U.S.A. that now are of "differing lingo background" would develop a unity with the rest of the citizens that is badly needed.

Martin Weston, a Knight Newspaper writer, told in the Charlotte *Observer* for October 14, 1971, of "the land where the Geechees and Gullahs live." To get to it, Weston had gone "up from Savannah through long tunnels of hanging Spanish moss and along single-lane blacktops dangerous from intermittent showers." The people he encountered in towns "like Ridgeland, Frogmore, and Okatie in South Carolina" where his ancestral cousins had lived speak Afro-American dialects called Geechee and Gullah. They live "substantially the way their fathers lived hundreds of years ago." On 63 sea islands in Beaufort County, 63 dialects were reported. It would be interesting to know how much they vary one from the other and from standard English. More interesting, however, to my wife and me, is the question, When will the bilingual program of education and culturalization that we had seen bearing priceless fruit among the Lezghians be carried out for the Geechees and Gullahs and other language groups of the U.S.A.? One gets the impression from Mr. Weston's frank and interesting article that such a program might not cost, in the long run, a great deal more than what is now spent on welfare.

CHAPTER X

A Visit to the Dargin Ethnic Group

It is not customary for foreigners to go to Mahachkala. The capital of Daghestan is not equipped with enough hotels to take care of very many outsiders and is therefore off the routes over which the Intourist Travel Agency is authorized to take you. Our first visit there was during the worst winter in two decades. Although we were in the "southern California" of the U.S.S.R. we had been greeted with a great deal of snow and ice everywhere in the Caucasus. Mahachkala was no exception, and when our train drew to a stop at the station near the shoreline of the Caspian Sea, a bitter wind was blowing. Someone said that it was from Siberia and we did not doubt it.

The hour was 3:30 A.M., and though our companions, Salim Melim, his wife, and granddaughter, were delightfully composed, we felt just a bit lost until a cordial man came quickly to where we were and welcomed us. His features, such as could be seen between the fur collar of his coat and his big warm cap, were strong and vibrant. Our welcomer was none other than the director of the Linguistic Institute, Gadji Danielov himself! His quiet, gracious wife had come with him in spite of the wicked weather and awful hour. We could not understand the animated conversation between her and Mme. Salim, but we could tell that it was cordial. The latter and her granddaughter were whisked away to the home of relatives, but the rest of us were taken downtown to the main hotel.

What a wonderful week followed! We met with scholars of the institute at a gathering presided over by Professor Danielov. They told us that archaeological evidence showed that the art of writing had existed in Daghestan as far back as the ninth century B.C. From the sixteenth century on, their little land of many tongues had produced some scientists and scholars who had attained recognition in the Middle East. The best of the cultural heritage left by them has been preserved, but it is in the Arabic language or at least in the Arabic script if perchance the learned man wrote in his own language. Today there are more than 14,000 teachers in Daghestan and 700 scientists with degrees. Also, 150 teachers of foreign languages have been sent back into the mountains to teach English, French, German, or Persian to youngsters whose grandparents could neither read nor write any language. In 1969 more than 300 Daghestanian young people were studying in Moscow State University. One of the seven delegates from the U.S.S.R. to a recent World Congress of Surgeons is a native of Daghestan, and his mother tongue is Goomik.

The president of the University of Daghestan appeared to be of Russian background, but the professors whom he assembled to meet with us were from several Daghestanian ethnic groups. One, whose father had been among the most outstanding early linguists and author of the dictionary of one of the Daghestanian languages, presented us with two of his father's linguistic books. When we mentioned in the discussion period that we felt the languages of Daghestan were important enough to merit having parts of the Bible translated into them, his reaction at first was negative, but when he realized that such an effort would not be proselyting and that Moslems admire the Bible, he was cordial.

I failed to count the number of Daghestanian languages represented at our conference, but there were several. Professor Murkelinsky, the author of the Lak-Russian dictionary, participated in one of our discussion groups. He, along with the patriarch, Salim Melim, was a veteran of the early days of the literacy drive, and it was easy to see how highly the younger men regarded him. We found that the linguists were well aware of up-to-date developments in the science of descriptive linguistics in other parts of the world. This was true also of the linguists of Tbilisi, Yerevan, and Baku. In fact, I felt so strongly the important potential of their contribution to the rest of the world of linguistic research that I suggested a linguistic conference be held sometime in one of those cities to which linguists of North and South America as well as Europe, Africa, Asia, and Australia might be invited. For one thing, a vast amount of worldwide comparative work needs to be done and linguists of the Caucasus could play important roles in this.

It was our privilege to dine with Professor and Mme. Danielov in their lovely cottage. They, like the Kasumkent teacher, had a private home rather than the customary apartment. It was surrounded by a spacious garden with fruit trees. The delicious food was Daghestanian as was also the warmth of friendship that prevailed around the feast-laden table, making us all forget the cold night outside.

I told our host that other multilanguage countries needed to know what had been accomplished in Daghestan and how it had been done. When I mentioned that there would be interest in a documentary film that told the story graphically from the time of the illiterate warring factions up to the present transformation, he informed me that one was being made. He arranged for us to see the work print of the film. We realized more than ever how many local language groups throughout the world could use a similar approach. The film does not play up or down any political ideology but simply shows a bit of the people as they were fifty years ago, especially their unique costumes, followed by the work of linguists; then that of educators, and terminates with the present triumph. The beautiful scenery of the country is not neglected. The man who was producing it seemed to be well trained and gifted artistically. I failed to ask him what language group he was from, but he was handling the subject as though he himself was a product of the program he was putting on the screen.

It was on our second visit, during October 1969, that Professor Danielov escorted us to the Dargin ethnic group. The trip had been impossible when we were with him the first time because the winter roads were unsafe. He had considered having a helicopter fly us, but the clouds over the mountains never did clear away sufficiently. In October, however, there was no problem. Professor Danielov himself directed the expedition that took us to the largest Dargin school and back in one long day.

Our road led north before it turned west to penetrate the foothills region. It skirted one town beautifully situated in a valley between ridges. A Moslem prayer tower was prominent near the center of the skyline. A new town had sprung up in another valley. We were told that it was inhabited by an ethnic group that had been moved there from a very isolated spot far back in the mountains. In another broad valley we saw a communal farm with its long apartment house for living quarters for the farmers and their families. Nearby were several hundred sheep feeding. Only one shepherd was in view, looking after the great herd. Evidently, system was stressed in farming also. In one barren area the hillside had been terraced to

The prayer tower of the mosque in this village along the highway to the Dargin area vies for attention with today's trucks, buses, cars, and attractive street lights in the foreground.

A communal farm between the Dargin area and the coast.

permit grain to be planted and irrigated. We had seen considerable irrigation along the seacoast where desert had been before. It was one of the economic developments that had accompanied the cultural revolution.

The Dargin school was in a large but plain brick building without fancy appointments. Anything fancy in the U.S.S.R. seems to be reserved for subway stations and bus stops where lovely art is lavished on the traveler. Otherwise, there is as little that savors of luxury as there was in the countryside of the U.S.A. when I was a boy sixty-five years ago. The school building faced a playground on two sides. On a third was a residential street near the center of town. We were taken to a reading class as well as to a class in which the pupils were making the transfer from Dargin to Russian. We also listened to older pupils recite in English. Again we noticed the orderliness of the classroom and the very evident application and ambition of the pupils. The teachers here as in most of the schools we visited were skillful at explaining to the children how to pronounce English and Russian.

In the Baku Primary School Number 90 we had observed a group of would-be teachers from the Pedagogical Institute listening to the pointers being given them in the practice classroom. Here in the Dargin school the principles and methodology were routine. These pupils were reciting in Russian and English but spoke Dargin at home and on the streets and listened to it on the radio. It was their language and they were proud of it, but *it was not going to get in the way of their progress.* Wise educators with the help of trained linguists were utilizing it as a tool toward the mastery of the only language that could unite them to the other peoples of the Caucasus and the entire U.S.S.R.

CHAPTER XI

Alphabets
in Saddlebags

As I looked at the snow-capped mountain ridges rising majestically far to the west of Kasumkent, I thought of what the literacy drive of the twenties and thirties must have cost the circuit-riding linguists and teachers. In those days dirt roads and trails became impassable during the wet season to everyone but expert horsemen. To cross a deep ravine from one village to another required hours of riding down one side and up the other. Also, upon arrival the language would be different, as well as some of the customs. In the twenties, if the circuit-riding teacher happened to be a woman, the people would be shocked because she wore no veil. Only gradually was parental permission granted for schoolgirls in Daghestan and Azerbaijan to remove their veils, and then they still had to wear scarves. In the case of one attractive woman school inspector in an area where daring young men had been accustomed to stealing a pretty girl for a wife, she had to take precautions against being stolen. Added to these obstacles was a dire lack of classrooms.

A community now nestles in the foothills near the coast, having moved from the high mountainous region of Daghestan. The paved highway keeps it in touch with the capital, Mahachkala, and opportunity.

The four features that overcame the problems were: (1) Everybody except the senior citizens *wanted* to learn to read. After all, the new day demanded it, and if some were too old to want to learn, the younger folks did want to and had such confidence in their excellence as an ethnic group that they were sure they could. (2) There were adequate numbers of young men and women who were willing to go wherever necessary, study several years to learn to teach, and then return to the mountains and establish good schools. (3) The government was willing to pay all the costs. (4) There was suitable methodology.

I had been aware of a fine school established in Mexico in the late twenties for the training of Indians from several language groups to become teachers and leaders, but it was closed after a few years because many of the graduates, it was said, refused to return to their tribal habitats to teach. My sus-

These schoolgirls in Daghestan during October 1969 are attired in warm clothing despite the area's reputation for a mild climate.

picion was that their not returning was due to the then prevailing lack of money to finance new schools and the lack of proper methodology. If some groups of North American Indians seem not to be adequately ambitious today to take on literacy and progress in the tremendous way the minority language groups of the Caucasus have, it is doubtless due in part to defects in the past system which have bred lack of confidence.

Certainly with the minority language groups of Latin America the ambition to learn is present when opportunity arrives. A barefoot friend of mine in an Aztec town near Mexico City told me of how, when he was still illiterate, the wind had blown part of a newspaper across the field to where he was planting beans. He stopped his work, and, longing to know what it said, put the paper to his ears. "How can some people hear what it says?" he wondered. Literacy classes in Aztec brought the answer. On the upper regions of the Urubamba River in Peru's vast Amazon region, all the men of a primitive village would cut short their labors or even their hunting expeditions to listen to two women, linguists of the Summer Institute of Linguistics, tell them how to "hear the paper talk."

On a visit to one of the Yagua tribal schools in Peru, I had noticed that some of the boys still used the attire that had fooled Orellana, the Spanish explorer who discovered the Amazon River. They wore skirts made of palm fiber and also headdresses of the same stuff that certainly made them look like women. I could understand why Orellana and his band of conquering Spaniards had thought that the warriors who opposed them were fighting women (Amazons) and had named the great river for them. What was engraved indelibly on my mind, though, about those Yagua boys was their thirst for knowledge. They would not take their eyes off the newly made and newly discovered reader even to hear the parrots scold from the giant trees above them. Why? *Why* did they want to read when in their jungle world there were no books, magazines, or newspapers? But learn they did, and already Peru is harvesting tremendous results from its bilingual schools among many tribes.

A humorous story has come down from Mexico's assault on illiteracy back in the early forties. The government had appealed to all literate citizens with the idea of "each one, teach one" to read. A villager went to market in a nearby city to sell his produce, and there he heard some men talking about the big news that those who knew how to read should teach people who did not know. He failed to get the point that each reader was to teach *one*. He thought that the knowledge was to be passed on to all the neighbors who lacked it. In his isolated hamlet there were fifteen men who could not read and only one who could. Even this percentage was better than in the Caucasus prior to Lenin. The man went home and told his neighbors what he had heard. They were thrilled inasmuch as everyone wanted to become literate. They soon got together, all fifteen of them, and marched to the home of the one literate. He was more prosperous than the rest and wore a pistol at his belt.

"Have you heard of the new law?" they asked. "The President of the Republic, President Avila Camacho, has decreed that all who know how to read should teach others. We have come for you to teach us. Please start right now!"

The man was amazed. "I'm no teacher," he said. "I can't teach. There's no use trying. Go home."

"But you must," they replied. "The President has decreed it. You have to teach us!"

"Get away!" the man cried as he rose to his feet and whipped out his pistol. "Get away from here or I'll shoot."

The would-be learners had to leave and wait.

Yes, the people of the Caucasus with their many languages had ambition and ability, and the government, prodded by the Revolution's basic emphasis on the liberty to learn in every man's mother tongue, held a steady course of bilingualism. Young men and women were trained to teach their own people first in their local language and then in Russian. As in the case of other groups Lezghians were sent for training to faraway Leningrad, Moscow, Rostov, or Kiev. They came back and taught the boys and girls of their own Lezghian "nationality" bilingually. Every kopek needed was provided. As with the Lezghians so also with other language groups if the speakers numbered 10,000 or more. Illiteracy was uprooted by the end of the forties, but the happy combination did not stop there. Professor R. Y. Yusifov, Sub-Director of the Daghestanian Scientific Research Institute for Schools, related the following to my associates, Dr. Esther Matteson and Mrs. Ann Eliza Tate:

> *I am the son of a day laborer. My parents were illiterate. I became a teacher in my home village [Lezghian]. I graduated from the Pedagogical Institute here in Mahachkala and now have a higher degree. My son graduated from Moscow State University and is a lawyer. My second son graduated from the University*

*here and is now a postgraduate student at Moscow
State University. My third son is a musician, the director
of a local music school. My daughter is a medical doctor.
In former times Daghestan had to ask for specialists to
come from Moscow. Now there are enough local specialists and so my daughter has gone to Siberia to practice
medicine there.*

*My wife is a teacher and works as director of a nurs-
ery. The wife of my oldest son is working on her Can-
didate of Science Degree, doing her research on creatures
of the sea. The wife of my second son has earned degrees
at the local university in both German and English and
now teaches at the university. The wife of my third son
is a history teacher. My daughter's husband, a native
speaker of the Lak language, is also a medical doctor.
Their sons are married, one to a Lezghian and the other
to a Russian girl.*

Apples on a sidewalk fruit stand in Tbilisi being observed by a Georgian student from the university across the street.

The director of the Daghestanian Scientific Research Institute for Schools, Professor Abduragim G. Sagidov, said that he started out as a teacher in a village school among the speakers of the Lak language, though neither his parents nor grandparents could read or write. There are 63,000 speakers of Lak. It was Professor G. Murkelinsky who, in 1938, gave them a Russian-based alphabet that simplified reading and writing greatly. The Laks have a newspaper, one magazine, books, radio and television programs, and schools in their own language. In one of their villages there is a secondary school with over 700 pupils.

Though forty years ago educators with brand-new alphabets and bilingual primers in their saddlebags were pioneers, Professor Sagidov told Dr. Matteson and Mrs. Tate that today "it is difficult to find a single family in all of Daghestan in which there is not at least one member with a higher education."

After teaching in a Lak school for some time, Professor Sagidov became Minister of Education for the entire Republic of Daghestan.

Now he is director of the institute in many-tongued Daghestan that conducts research on methodology and prepares textbooks in the local languages. Dr. Matteson and Mrs. Tate asked him how the system of bilingual education worked and the part his institute played in it. His answers made clear the following points:

> *The purpose of the Daghestanian Scientific Research Institute for Schools is to carry on scientific research for the benefit of schools in the indigenous languages, to prepare textbooks and programs, and work out teaching methods. There are three departments of the institute: (1) Daghestanian languages with separate sections for Avar, Lak, Lezghian, Dargin, Kumik, Tabasaran; (2) the Russian language; (3) pedagogical and methodological work.*
> *The department of Daghestanian languages has sci-*

entists doing research in each of the languages on how to teach in the bilingual [national-local language] schools. Books are published in each of the six local languages used, as well as in Russian. The institute has its own printing department where any book written and approved is printed without delay.

The scientist who makes the book is always a native speaker of the language. Recently, members of the institute met with members of the Academy of Science to work out a common terminology. Each of the languages requires some special symbols, and each alphabet therefore differs somewhat from the others. The Russian has thirty-three symbols; the highest number of symbols or letters in a Daghestanian language is forty-seven.

Textbooks for the various languages are not translated from Russian or some other language but are prepared entirely from the very start for a particular language and people. Those who prepare the books in a given language are native speakers of that language, as are all those who work in the schools, teachers of Russian, English, French, etc., as well as teachers of subjects in the native languages. Even though villages are similar culturally, pictures in the books are typical of the region where the book is to be used. For example, books for mountain villages show two-story stone houses, while those for schools in the plains show one-story houses made of locally used materials.

The principles set forth by Professor Sagidov have been followed to a certain degree in other parts of the world, and they have worked there too. What I have yet to find anywhere outside the U.S.S.R., however, is an institution such as the Daghestanian Scientific Research Institute for Schools, which is composed exclusively of experts who come from the very minority language groups that are being served. All multi-language countries need them, but it will take years to prepare experts like Sagidov to man them.

CHAPTER XII

Putting Babel
in Reverse

If the schools of the Caucasus have been quick to teach in the local tongues, not so the mosques and churches. Services in the mosques are conducted in foreign, though "sacred," Arabic, the language of the Koran. Liturgy in the churches of Armenia has been given in a long-forgotten form of Armenian. The man in the street does not understand either Arabic or ancient Armenian.

One of the high officials in the Academy of Science at Yerevan took us to visit the Catolicos, or head prelate of the Armenian Catholic Church. His headquarters are at Echmiadzin, a few miles from Yerevan. The Catolicos, who had just returned from a visit to Armenian Church centers in the U.S.A., received us most graciously. While our conversation with him progressed we were served some of the best cake I ever ate. Then he invited us to accompany him to the big church where mass was about to be celebrated. The modern flavor prevalent in all the schools we had visited was lacking in the church. The very evident fervor and the music were in-

Classroom in Tasumkent. The Lezghian alphabet is now based on the Russian alphabet, as are all those of Daghestan.

spiring and we were thankful for the liberty of worship, but we wondered at the contrast between church and school. The same had been true at a Russian Orthodox Church we attended in Moscow, except that there the language was not ancient Armenian but ancient Russian or Church Slavonic.

Attitudes as well as the liturgy savored of the past. In an old church in Tbilisi, Georgia, we saw a woman kissing the floor and a wooden coffin as her ancestors had done for centuries.

We were glad to learn when we were in Echmiadzin that in the church publishing house a block or two from the church, the modern version of the Bible was being printed. We also rejoiced when we were told by Baptist ministers in Moscow that the Baptist churches had received from the Soviet Government an edition of thousands of copies of the Bible in their favorite version that, if not strictly up-to-date, is at least in much more modern Russian than the English of the King James Version.

The most prosperous farmers of the Caucasus are said to be grape growers in Armenia and Georgia.

An Armenian linguist gave us quite a jolt when he stated that even the modern literary Armenian language in which the Bible is being printed is not the native tongue of all of the two million Armenians living within the confines of that little republic nor of the million and a half Armenians living in other parts of the U.S.S.R., mainly Georgia and Azerbaijan. Sixty dialects are spoken in different areas, and even the dialect used in the capital city differs a bit from eastern literary Armenian.

We received the impression that not nearly so much has been done linguistically in the village schools of Armenia as in Daghestan. A friend from Moscow told us that she was traveling recently by train from Yerevan to Baku and at a village many miles from Yerevan but still in Armenia she found that *no one* could talk with her in Russian. This would not have happened in Daghestan in any town traversed by the railroad or highway, and possibly not anywhere in that state except in the mountainous areas most difficult of access.

The snow-covered saddleback peaks of Mt. Ararat across the border in Turkey were hidden by clouds all the time we were in Yerevan. The interesting paperback entitled *Armenia*, published by the Novosti Press in Moscow, encourages travelers with the following statement about the high valley in which Yerevan is situated: "The number of sunny days in the area of . . . the Ararat Valley (310-320 days per year) almost equal those of Egypt (the Alexandria area) and Central Asia (Termez)."

We did not experience any sunny days but expect to do so when we return. One unforgettable view of Mt. Ararat that we did enjoy, however, was when our plane broke through the clouds when we were leaving Yerevan. We could imagine Noah's ark resting in the saddle between the high and low peaks. Somewhere, not too many days of horseback-riding away, might well have been the site of Babel where the first

Landscape of Mt. Ararat by famous Armenian painter, M. Sarian.
Novosti Press Agency

multiplication of tongues took place. Over the centuries further multiplication, by natural processes, occurred. One Armenian tongue became sixty, and the one original Lezghian tongue in Daghestan became ten. That small republic's total bequest from Babel, whether five or thirty, became sixty-eight or, as some say, over a hundred. Not until Lenin and his successors began honoring each man's mother tongue and using it as a steppingstone to the knowledge of a common tongue was Babel put in reverse there in the Caucasus.

The slower progress of bilingual education among most of the dialects of Armenia may be attributed, as in Daghestan, to the fact that many of the dialects have seemed to be spoken by too few to merit the usual approach. Some are spoken by only a few hundred people. Just two of the ten dialects of Lezghian are written and used in the schools. Where separate languages are spoken by only one or two villages, the children are generally taught in the major language of the area. Non-Lezghian villages that are next-door neighbors of the Lezghians are taught in that language, since there are no books in their own tongue. If their own happens to be a dialect of Lezghian, the problem is not so great as when the language is completely different. In the latter case, the parents may request that instruction begin right from the start in Russian.

There are linguists who feel that the small groups did not ask for their own writing systems because "in linguistic, cul-

A teacher in a Tbilisi school. On the bulletin board behind her in her office appear pictures of children who made some outstanding contribution to the program. Smiling at her left stands the president of the Pioneer Club, an organization in which pupils are trained for possible future party membership.

Schoolchildren have very heavy study schedules and no inter-school athletics, but they appear to be a happy lot. These youngsters in Tbilisi are bilingual (Georgian and Russian) but typically Georgian in appearance and quite distinctive from the Daghestanian, Azerbaijanian, and Armenian types.

tural, and economic attitudes they find themselves under the influence of other groups of larger population." In their own languages they communicate among themselves within the limits of their villages, but their languages do not serve as a means of communication with the other inhabitants of the region and of the republic in which they live. The supposition is that they are somewhat bilingual not in Russian but in the language of a neighboring group in which there are school books for at least the first three grades. It is not surprising that parents would just as soon have their children skip the neighboring language and go right after the language of their cosmonaut heroes, but it did surprise me that the fine linguistic and educational machine that has been built up in the Caucasus had not prepared textbooks in the tongues of the real small

Village women of Armenia in local garb. *Novosti Press Agency*

groups. A linguist reassured us, saying: "If some small national group is not bilingual, then, in spite of the small number, a writing system would be prepared for that group in its native language. On the basis of this principle, writing systems were provided for extremely small national groups of the north, such as Nany, Eskimo, and others."

We were told that there are fifteen written languages in the Caucasus of which twelve could be called "newly written," i.e., written during the past fifty years. For all of the U.S.S.R., according to the book, *Recently Written Languages,* alphabets have been provided for all languages with 10,000 or more speakers. A nationality as small as the Abkhazian (59,000, or about two-thirds the size of the Navajo tribe) has in its own difficult form of speech, not only its own system of writing but also newspapers, radio and television programs, books, theatricals, laws, songs, poems, primary and secondary schools, and two institutes.

Professor Y. D. Desheriev outlined the linguistic program in the entire U.S.S.R. with its seventy written languages and numerous unwritten ones as follows:

1. *Languages which have the widest social functions such as Azerbaijani, Armenian, Georgian, Ukranian, Belorussian, Moldavian, Lithuanian, Latvian, Estonian, Turkmen, Tadzik, Uzbek, were to have elementary, secondary, and higher educational institutions.*

2. *Languages such as Tatar, Bashkir, Chulash, Udmurd, Karakalak, Finno-Ugrian, were to have primary and secondary schools but were to be used little in higher educational institutions. Scientific works were limited to those of a popular nature. These languages have their own newspapers, journals, fiction, theaters, radio, television, etc.*

3. *Languages such as Ykut, Osetic, Abkhaz, were to be used in primary and incomplete secondary schools (seven or eight grades). In science, these have only school books and popular works. They have, however, newspapers, radio, television, theaters, fiction, dictionaries, and journals.*

4. *Languages of very small groups such as Chukot and Eskimo with only a few thousand speakers each, whose members are not bilingual with larger groups, were to have writing systems and primary schools. There are, however, very few newspapers, fiction works, and textbooks. In response to the desires of the small groups themselves, education in the higher grades is provided in the greater languages.*

5. *Languages of very small groups whose members are bilingual were not to have writing systems or schools. For them all written materials and education would be in the language of the national republic to which they belong. For example, the Xinalog are taught in Azerbaijani, the Batsbi in Georgian, etc.*

Dr. Matteson, after visiting several schools in Mahachkala, Baku, and other cities of the Caucasus, adds:

> *In all parts of the Caucasus and at all levels language learning is prominent. Secondary schools and language institutes typically have the finest modern equipment. One example is an English language classroom in a secondary school with a large control panel on the instructor's desk from which she could speak privately with any member of her class, direct a tape recording or record player to him alone, assign any two in separate parts of the room to converse together, and monitor as she wished.*

Where does the money come from to equip such a program? Where did the money come from to prepare the teachers who use the equipment? In the U.S.S.R. it comes from the State, but in other parts of the world other sources have been tapped to a degree. A Roman Catholic priest in Colombia, South America, has conducted literacy classes by radio for many years. He needed inexpensive radio receivers for the learners, and on one occasion secured a grant of money from a commercial firm. With money in hand, he went to Japan and bought satisfactory sets in large numbers for less than ten dollars apiece. Such donations from commercial firms and foundations should be sought wherever possible, but the main financial burden must be borne by concerned governments as it is in the Caucasus.

CHAPTER XIII

Imperialism
or Essential Service?

If you were to go from Moscow to the Caucasus by train or car, the shortest route would take you through the charming, fairly large city of Sochi on the northeastern shore of the Black Sea. It is famous as a health resort and has many sanatoriums belonging mostly to labor organizations all over the U.S.S.R. Good accommodations are available for a fair number of tourists, and if you are interested in beautiful scenery, boat rides on historic waters, a semitropical climate, and tea plantations, you could probably get reservations by calling on your nearest Intourist agent. An airport is relatively close to the city. It is reached by following the shoreline on a picturesque highway leading south. Aeroflot Soviet Airlines would be the way to go from Moscow or Rostov.

An exotic language had been spoken formerly in the mountains nearby, but that was not the reason why we went to Sochi. The high official at the Academy of Science in Moscow who planned our trip felt that we should have a special treat after our tour of study and routed us that way.

We did see, however, linguistic science in action. At one of the big city schools we were asked if we would like to listen to a class of first graders that was about to receive its English lesson. We of course said yes, and were led across the patio to a classroom where good-looking, well-dressed seven year olds were gathering. Some of the children greeted us courteously with well-spoken good mornings. We were reminded of older youngsters whom we had met on the train the day before as we had followed the shoreline from Sukhumi far to the south. They too had greeted us in English and with warm smiles. The teacher was a neatly dressed young woman under twenty-five years of age. She was a graduate of a teachers' training center at Rostov. Her manner was very businesslike. The youngsters followed her every move with the closest attention. It was only their seventh lesson since starting from scratch, but they had learned to say a number of expressions quite well. She drilled them for awhile on these. Then she took them through a series of well-selected exercises to drill them on pronunciation. At one point she had them all bring out small mirrors and watch their mouths as she told them where to put their tongues in relationship to their lips, teeth, or roof of the mouth. The cooperation of the seven year olds was perfect.

We appreciated that experience, but there was another one that transcended it, one that had nothing to do with either linguistics or bilingual education. I refer to the International Friendship Tree of Sochi, which we visited, for friendship is the language of the heart. Inasmuch as we were guests of the Academy of Science, I was asked to graft a bud onto a sister tree, since the original Friendship Tree already had more than a full quota of citrus varieties.

We stopped at Sochi again when we were in the Caucasus a second time. We were received at the Friendship Tree by the mayor's representative and four citizens who were members

The agronomist in charge of the International Friendship Tree on the Experimental Farm for Subtropical and Thermophillic Plants in Sochi holds guest book open to page on which appear the signatures of U. N. Under-Secretary General for Special Political Affairs Ralph J. Bunche and industrialist Cyrus Eaton of Cleveland. Forty-five varieties of citrus fruit now grow on the Friendship Tree on which visitors from 125 countries have made grafts. Soil has been sent from many places to be sprinkled over the roots as a symbol of friendship, prompting Ralph Bunche to write in the guest book: "In friendship are the roots of peace." Soil from Illinois, the Land of Abraham Lincoln, was sprinkled over the roots by Dr. Townsend.

In October 1969 Dr. and Mrs. Townsend pose before the International Friendship Tree in Sochi. It bears yellow lemons, oranges, grapefruit, pompelmous, and kin kan tangerines. During the Townsends' earlier visit in February of that year it was covered over with plastic into which warm air was pumped on cold nights.

of the International Friendship Committee. Their president, a delightful woman, joined us for a ceremony at which she presided. In my speech I quoted Benito Juárez to the effect that respect for the rights of others is peace. Then we presented a small silver box full of soil from the Land of Abraham Lincoln. In our imagination, Juárez and Lincoln, who in their lifetime were personal friends, watched as I sprinkled some of the rich Illinois loam around the roots of the main tree. On the lid of the silver box was a photoengraved picture of the great emancipator that had been made for the occasion by a friend, a photoengraver of Charlotte, North Carolina. The box was placed on display in the Friendship Museum.

The day before, the same committee had had a similar ceremony in which U.N. Under-Secretary General for Special Political Affairs Ralph J. Bunche and industrialist Cyrus Eaton of Cleveland had participated. We looked at their signatures in the guest book at the museum and were deeply moved as we read what Cyrus Eaton had written above his signature. It was an adaptation from the last book of the Bible, the book of Revelation: "May the leaves of the tree be for the healing of the nations."

The healing of friendship! I thought of how greatly our troubled world needed such leaves and dared to hope for the day when these Biblical words would be translated into every language.

We had come out of the Caucasus at the Black Sea gateway where ordinarily we would have entered. From Sochi we looked back in our memories upon a rugged area that had existed for centuries fragmented not only by mountains and streams but also by divergent tongues, cultures, and selfish interests. Today it stands united to a remarkable degree. Before it had been only as strong as a splintered oak; today it has the might of oneness. Now the vast stores of scientific literature of Moscow, Leningrad, and the City of Science in Siberia lie within its grasp. Before, except for the favored few, there were no books in the local tongues, and people could not have read them had they existed.

After returning to the United States I wrote an article with some of the foregoing information and enthusiasm and showed it to a university professor in the Midwest, a specialist on countries near the U.S.S.R. He wrote me as follows when he returned the manuscript:

> *This is an interesting, personal account of the Azerbaijanian people. Their advances over the past fifty years have been very impressive and evidently much of their progress can be attributed to the teaching of both the native and Russian languages. Learning the languages provided the people with vehicles for mastering the basic trades and professional skills that improve the quality of life in a society.*
>
> *Since you are a linguist who sees in human communications a means of overcoming barriers that separate peoples and a means of permitting individuals to develop their individual talents, you can appreciate the advances in Azerbaijan more than many people in the world. I can sympathize with your viewpoint and am also impressed with the achievements.*
>
> *However, for anyone who is unfavorably disposed toward the Soviet Union, teaching the Russian language to all the nationalities in the U.S.S.R. would be viewed as a sophisticated form of imperialism. The language is the first step in a Russification program—a program which the czars attempted to perpetrate but failed whereas the Communists attempted and succeeded.*

I realize my position will be questioned by some, but in reply I would ask: Should literacy and economic and social progress in the Caucasus have stopped short of unification or should unification have come around a language other than Russian? Should the many language groups have picked Georgian or Armenian around which to rally and unite? Would

Pronunciation drill in an English class in the Caucasus.

that have not been open to criticisms as just another form of imperialism, though a more local one? What chance would a boy of one of the small language groups of Daghestan have of becoming a cosmonaut if he did not know the Russian language? What chance does a Puerto Rican boy in a ghetto of New York City have of becoming an outstanding scientist if he does not learn English well or cannot afford to go to a country where he can study in Spanish?

The average citizen of the U.S.A. does not realize the serious language problem that exists in his own land. In the first chapter of this book I have quoted from the "Bilingual Education Act" of Congress of January 2, 1968. The quotation states that the problem involves "millions of children of limited English-speaking ability because they come from environments where the dominant language is other than English."

Would it be imperialistic to give these youngsters within the confines of the U.S.A. a proper mastery of the English language? Many French Canadians would complain if their children were taught English as a second language as systematically as Russian is taught in the Caucasus, but Canada would become stronger and the French Canadian young people would have more opportunities. What about the Navajos, Papagos, Apaches, and many other minority language groups? Is it too late to use the bilingual approach with them? The U.S. Congress has appropriated funds for concerned educators in the country to work with. Will they learn the methodology that has worked for the U.S.S.R.? Will they have the determination to carry it out? The future of the "millions of children" who come from "environments where the dominant language is other than English" depends upon it.

Years ago a greatly concerned Mexican writer, Miguel Othón de Mendizábal, in relating some of the accomplishments of linguists and educators in the Caucasus and other parts of the U.S.S.R., pondered the same questions. "It is difficult to prognosticate," he wrote, "whether the great allied nations will know in the future how to take advantage of this great social policy."*

If anyone had sensed a humiliating imperialism, it would have been my friend Othón de Mendizábal. To the contrary, he wrote approvingly of the policy of giving "the small nationalities" an autonomous setup,

> . . . *developing and consolidating their own tribunals, their own administrative and economic organizations, their own political and social life and, to sum it up, employing their mother tongues under the direction of native leaders well acquainted with the customs and psychology of the people to introduce and promote among them newspapers, theaters, clubs and all the means of cultural diffusion. All was to be in their own languages. In these same languages, coordinated systems*

* *Complete Works of Miguel Othón de Mendizábal* (Mexico City: Talleres Graficos de la Nacion, 1946), Vol. 4, p. 393.

*of schools and institutes were to be established but the
Russian tongue and foreign languages were to be used
as well both in the primary grades and for imparting
social, technical and professional knowledge.* *

Othón de Mendizábal went on to give data concerning the
herculean task of providing "linguistically, pedagogically and
editorially" teaching materials in many different languages for
2,753,292 students in the Caucasus and Central Asia (data is
thirty years old). He terminated one of his articles by saying:

> *I do not ignore nor can anyone else ignore the tech-
> nical and financial problems as well as the political and
> social resistance that such a tremendous pedagogical
> change would imply to Mexico.*
>
> *It behooves our Mexican philologists and the foreign
> linguists who collaborate with them so unselfishly [mem-
> bers of the Summer Institute of Linguistics mainly] as
> well as our teachers to carry out the necessary investi-
> gations and experiments that will enable the Ministry of
> Education . . . to change the present direction of public
> education insofar as it concerns the people where Indian
> languages are spoken.* * *

The millions of Indians in Mexico, Peru, Bolivia, Ecuador,
Guatemala and other Spanish-speaking countries *can* learn the
national language and learn it well. They are capable. But it is
necessary to train thousands of them to teach their fellow
tribesmen with the expertise shown by the young lady we
watched teaching in Sochi. They will learn. Only then will the
peoples of those lands, not to mention many more on other
continents, become truly unified. With unity comes progress
and power.

* Ibid., p. 180.
* * Ibid., p. 181.

CHAPTER XIV

Language Barriers
in Other Lands

As long as in the same nation some people have all the
technical advantages of education and science while
others in large numbers exist without even an alphabet,
social peace will be but a mocking mirage.
                                        —Jaime Torres Bodet.

Twenty-five years have passed since Othón de Mendizábal
wrote his ponderings over the gigantic step that Mexico would
have to take if it were going to bring all of its 130 minority
language groups out of illiteracy and linguistic isolation into
the full heritage of the fatherland. There has been no attempt
to establish an Autonomous Tarahumara Republic or a Sub-
sidiary Republic of Yucatan with laws, newspapers, and radio
programs all in the Tarahumara or Mayan languages and with
the first three grades of the primary schools taught in the
same tongues. It is not likely that that aspect of the Caucasus
example has been given any serious consideration whatever,
and I do not believe that Othón de Mendizábal thought it
was even a possibility. There has been considerable bilingual

education, however, based on the findings of linguistic research.

Experiments began on a small scale in Mexico soon after the First Philological Assembly was held in Mexico City in 1939 and received greater impulse during the first term of Jaime Torres Bodet as Minister of Education in the forties. In the law that set up a great nationwide drive for literacy in 1944 there was a provision that called for bilingual primers in Indian languages and in Spanish. When Torres Bodet accepted the leadership of UNESCO in 1948, he held an international conference in Paris to deal with, for one thing, the need of linguistic research and bilingual education in various parts of the world.

During Torres Bodet's second term as Mexico's Minister of Education (1958-1964) the program of bilingual education grew until, under his successor Agustín Yañez, over 2,500 bilingual teachers (*promotores*) representing several important Indian languages had been assigned to the task. Many thousands of Indians have learned to read both in their own tongues and in Spanish. Furthermore, one team of linguists in the State of Chiapas trained thirty men in one language group to practice medicine in areas where there had been no doctor. The Indians have come also into a new understanding and appreciation of the fatherland.

Peru's revolutionary government came out officially for bilingual education early in 1971. Back in 1952 when General Juan Mendoza was Minister of Education, a very important step in this direction had been taken by the founding of a Teachers' Training Course for Jungle Indians right in the heart of Peru's Amazon forest. Ever since then more and more Indian teachers speaking jungle languages have been trained and commissioned to go back to their own language areas and teach. Some 250 bilingual schools have been established where thousands of children, just one or two generations removed from savagery, have learned to read and write in their own unique languages and then in Spanish. Some have gone on to schools of higher learning in the cities.

Over thirty languages are spoken in Peru's forested hinterland, but the speakers of most of them number only a few thousand in each case. In the Andean highlands, however, there are millions of Quechua speakers, and the government began a bilingual teaching program among them a few years ago when the editor and philosopher, Francisco Miró Quesada, was Minister of Education. He himself wrote a prologue for the Quechua primers in May 1964, in which he said, among other things:

> *It is evident that any child in any part of the world finds it better to learn to read in the language of his own community rather than in a language that is forced upon him. The proofs, however, that have been established by patient scientific labor become exigencies. The findings which are the fruit of the labors of the Summer Institute of Linguistics and of all the research that its linguists carry on in many places throughout the vast forest are indisputable and final. Technically the first steps in education should be in the language that the pupil as well as his family and his village speaks. The process of learning is more rapid, more permanent, and more natural. Once the pupil has learned to read in his own language he can then move on to the official language [Spanish, in Peru] with surprising efficacy. . . . The technique, however, is not the only aspect. To start teaching a child in his own mother tongue has a more far-reaching significance than just the utilization of a methodology. Above all, it means recognition. It means that the child's language is not considered inferior or detestable. It means that in Peru at long last the barrier, formed by the feeling of Indian inferiority, is breaking down. When this happens, many other things happen, each one more surprising. One of them has taken place already: the comprehension shown by the groups that*

*are the objects of the new approach. The way in which
they have received the new methods . . . the transformation of the process of education into flesh of their
flesh, is startling. . . . The teachers have been received
with expressive jubilance.*

Other countries of Latin America that have the problem of
illiterate minority language groups have watched the program of bilingual education in Mexico and Peru with keen
interest and several have initiated similar programs. Guatemala has trained Indians to teach their own people. Ecuador
has written into its constitution a provision that establishes
the right of its numerous Indian inhabitants to learn in their
own tongues. As far as I know, Ecuador is the only country
in the Western Hemisphere to have given constitutional status
to the highly praiseworthy but very difficult project. Definite
progress has been made toward the attainment of the goal.

The status of bilingual education in still other Latin American lands is mostly in the research and experimental stage.
Even in Paraguay, where both Spanish and Guaraní are official national languages and bilingualism in speaking those
two languages is quite general, little stride had been made in
bilingual education. Several Indian languages are spoken
monolingually in the Gran Chaco part of Paraguay, however,
and the government is considering the assignment of linguists
to work on them. Panama has already done this for its language
groups and before long should be initiating bilingual education. Colombia and Bolivia have made some important head-
way with the assistance of dedicated linguists, but Peru and
Mexico are still far ahead of them. In Peru, where there was
almost complete illiteracy in most jungle language groups
twenty-five years ago, can now be found not only numerous
readers, schools, and Indian teachers but also Indian outboard
engine mechanics, agronomists, merchants, carpenters, practical doctors, nurses, and town officials. They are results of
the bilingual approach.

When we were in the Philippines, I was informed that the Ivatan language group, living on three islands north of Luzon, is one of the most literate groups in the Philippines and that this is due to truly bilingual and dedicated teachers. Young Ivatan natives went to Manila for an education and returned to teach their own people. Not until quite recently were there any textbooks in the Ivatan language, but all along explanations were given and problems discussed in Ivatan by native Ivatan teachers. This helped greatly, and I was told that "from these three small islands have come teachers, lawyers, judges, doctors, and linguists by scores, not to mention military officers and craftsmen as well as farmers who rank among the most industrious of the Philippines. Almost without exception the Ivatan children attend school at least through grade three, most of them through grade six, and many through high school and on into college." Their teachers in the early years also spoke the Ivatan language. The official language of the Philippine Republic since 1936 has been Pilipino, otherwise known as Tagalog, but local languages such as Ivatan may be utilized to promote its use.

In Australian New Guinea linguists have worked in more than 100 of its 700 languages and, generally, with promising success. Two young women, Mary Stringer and Joyce Hotz, wrote to me about the Waffa people whose language they have studied for several years. As soon as they had established the phonemics of the language, they worked out an alphabet in which there was only one symbol for one sound and one sound for one symbol. This type of alphabet is called a phonemic alphabet. The Spanish alphabet, for example, is almost phonemic. The alphabets now used in Daghestan and most other parts of the Caucasus are phonemic or nearly so. Linguists who give alphabets to languages for the first time are generally careful to make them strictly phonemic. This is one basic reason why children can learn to read them in two or three months' time, whereas in a nonphonemically written language such as English or French many children require two years or longer to learn to read, if then.

Of course Mary Stringer and Joyce Hotz gave the Waffas a phonemic alphabet. They made primers, and began literacy classes as their time permitted. Now *all the young people* are literate in both the vernacular and the trade language, Pidgin. It is unnecessary for the linguists to give them classes in the latter. They automatically transfer to Pidgin the sound values they learned in Waffa, and it works. There is also a strong motivation to learn to read the language that enables them to communicate with other tribesmen, and that helps greatly.

Trained teachers in large numbers are needed for any massive literacy and bilingual educational movement. I know an Indian medical doctor from Guatemala who attained her education after she was thirteen years of age. Until that time she could neither read nor write, though she was brilliant. Today she is emergency surgeon at a large hospital. She is an encouragement to government educators who want to see her large language group, the Quiches, progress, but working long hours as a surgeon leaves her no time to teach her people to read.

On the other hand, I know a Mexican Indian who did not become literate until after he was ten and who went on to learn five more languages while studying in Mexico City and abroad. In fact, he earned his master's degree under an international scholarship to a university in Germany. The important thing, as far as his tribe is concerned, is that he, their fellow Totonac Indian, returned to Mexico and started an institute for his people with classes conducted in their own Totonac language. He is training young men who speak the Totonac language as their mother tongue to teach others of their people.

Any country, therefore, that really wants to educate its minority language groups must not only prepare enough teachers, but it must also pay them adequately. Some of the

One of the new university buildings erected some distance from the center of Tbilisi.

better-educated Indian teachers can get along on the low salaries ordinarily paid rural schoolteachers, but others cannot. The higher they go in the scale of education the more valuable they can become to the group-transformation program we are analyzing, but the more their living will cost.

For example, I recently heard of an Indian boy in the highlands of South America who was monolingual in his Indian tongue. The classes that were given in Spanish in the little village school he attended were of no benefit to him. Other children like him learned after two years to read though not to understand Spanish. Then most of them would give up the thought of further schooling. Jaime, as we shall call the lad, was ambitious, however, and he continued to work hard until he could understand and speak Spanish too. Then he somehow was able to go to the capital city and study more. Eventually, the way was opened for him to study in the mother country, Spain. There he found that as in the Indian areas of his homeland, large sectors of the population also spoke other languages than Spanish, such as Catalán and Basque, and no one made fun of them. In fact, those languages were used in the classroom right through the university. Why, he wondered, had a Spanish viceroy during Peru's colonial period ordered the Quechuas to give up their language within six months and start speaking only Spanish? Why had his own teachers poked fun at him when he had absent-mindedly reverted to his own language in their presence? Why had it been impossible for him and his fellows to receive classes in their own language? Why had it been a case of learning in Spanish or not learning at all, and with the latter result for most of his friends?

Jaime returned to his homeland anxious to do something for his people, but a position was offered him at a highland university as professor of Spanish literature. He took it and was thus unable to do much for his people until the officials of the Ministry of Education made him director of a summer training course for Quechua Indian teachers. It was a superb opportunity for him to use his training and ability to help the movement to apply at least some of the basic principles that have been used so successfully in the Caucasus, but it did not last very long. I do not know for sure what happened; probably his salary was inadequate and Jaime moved to Lima. Bilingual teachers must be utilized as well as trained.

I have seen tears in the eyes of General Lázaro Cárdenas when he was president of Mexico, as he observed a group of Otomi Indians in their dire need. Who knew better than he, who had Indian blood in his own veins, and was proud of it, that in their number there were potential schoolteachers, doctors, and even statesmen if they could but overcome the barriers, linguistic and otherwise, that held them back? Today some of the Otomis do have bilingual textbooks, bilingual teachers, more land to till and irrigation water to make it produce. There are Otomis who have gone to the top.

Two Australian associates, one a linguist, took me to call on one of the highest officials in the educational program of the Northwest Territory of Australia. It was not the time of day when he was supposed to be there but he was, for he was deeply concerned. He and his staff of educators had worked for years on the theory that the 300 small language groups of aborigines (150 of the languages mutually unintelligible) could be unified linguistically by substituting their own languages with English. The method they had employed was to have the children start school at three and a half or four years of age and for the teachers to drill English into their little heads all day long. The government had enough money to secure the teachers and the school population was very small so that the chances of success seemed good, but the final results were unsatisfactory. For one thing, the youngsters heard poor and limited English in their homes, since the parents were told not to speak to them in the local tongue. This offset the good English they heard from the teachers. The result too often was that the children did not learn either the local tongue or English properly. They became people without a language, or rather people with such an inferior way of expressing themselves that they would be looked upon as inferior by both the settlers and their fellow aborigines the rest of their lives.

One investigator wrote:

> . . . the method of teaching English directly to non-English speakers without using the latters' language as a medium, has not proved as successful as was hoped. It is satisfactory for the first year or two with reference to concrete objects and situations. To go further, however, a bridge is needed between indigenous concepts and those the teacher seeks to introduce; and unless the local

*language be used as the main structure of that bridge,
the children are apt to flounder and seem unable to go
beyond rote achievement.* *

Naturally, a change had to be made and the Australian
official we were calling on was seriously considering the
bilingual approach. He saw problems, however, and they
weighed heavily on his mind. I shall never forget the deep
concern that that high official showed.

There is need for the U.S.A. to awaken to its own problem.
I do not refer only to the millions of children who cannot
speak English properly but also to the millions who cannot
read functionally. The report given to President Nixon's National Reading Council on September 10, 1970, indicated,
within the margins of statistical error, that as many as 18.5
million Americans over the age of sixteen are functionally
illiterate. They cannot read, comprehend, and answer such
questions as "Do you expect to incur any medical expenses
within the next three months?" * *

At least one bilingual experiment is under way to solve the
language problem and it is bound to help. According to an
article that appeared in the Los Angeles *Times* on December
11, 1969, it seemed likely that the "only truly bilingual public
school educational program in the United States" was found in
Texas at the Nye Elementary School in the rural United Con-
solidated School District of Webb County. "The children from
grades one to five . . . are taught all their classes, reading,
writing and arithmetic, in English and in Spanish concur-
rently." The District Superintendent, Harold C. Brantley,
"makes it clear that helping the Mexican-American child enter
the mainstream of the dominant culture and the dominant
language of the country is very important."

* A. P. Elkin, "Aboriginal Languages and Assimilation," *Oceania*, 1964,
No. 34, 149-150.
* * James J. Kilpatrick editorial, Charlotte *Observer*, Sept. 26, 1970.

With regard to the Mexican-American and other areas of the U.S.A. where a language besides English is spoken extensively, the *Times* article quotes the chief of the Mexican-American affairs unit of the U.S. Office of Education, Armando Rodriguez, as saying, "This country has assumed the monocultural and monolingual role for generations. We have always stripped our immigrants of their language and culture and expected them to conform to our customs and traditions."

In other words, it has been a case of substituting English for the local language instead of duplicating the local language with the national tongue as is done in the Caucasus.

In a statement concerning the speakers of American Indian languages, Douglas H. Latimer of Harper & Row's American Indian publishing program said in November, 1971: "The rate of alcoholism and suicide among the young people of many Indian tribes is appallingly high. One of the reasons for this is the terrible cultural shock experienced by the children when they first go to school. Many of these children on reservations have little or no knowledge of English when they first begin their education. Since their classes are taught entirely in English, it generally is at least a year or two before the children have learned enough English even to understand what is going on around them. . . . The Navahos have established an experimental school at Rough Rock, Arizona, which has predominantly Navaho teachers. Everything is taught in the Navaho language, using books written by Navahos for the first four years of the curriculum. Following this basic grounding in their own culture, the children then learn English as a second language for the next four years. Then they attend a high school in which their education is bilingual. Although the Rough Rock school has been in existence for only about six years, its results so far have been very encouraging."*

---

* Quoted from "Footnotes," house organ of Harper & Row.

CHAPTER XV

The Future of
Minority Language Groups

One of the main problems that confronted the deeply concerned educator in Australia's Northwest Territory was English spelling. Linguists had assured him that to teach the aborigines to read in their own languages was no great problem when these were reduced to writing. In the few languages where this work had been done the linguists had been careful, of course, to write them phonemically so that a person of average intelligence could learn to read them in a month or two. It was difficult, however, for them to read English with its terribly nonphonemic alphabet. The tribes were so small that it was hopeless to think of preparing much educational material for them beyond literacy booklets in their own tongues even if there should become available a sufficient number of linguists to do the work. A rapid transfer would have to be made to English for the essential schooling to become possible.

We have seen how easy it is for people to pass from literacy in their own local language to reading in the national language

A sidewalk bookstand in Tbilisi. Elaine Townsend and the representative of the Academy of Science in Tbilisi observe the selection and
prices of books. The many bookstores do not satisfy the demand and
therefore in most of the cities visited by the Townsends there were also
stands on the sidewalks and in the subways. Books were inexpensive and
serious. There was no pornography or drama emphasizing sex. Nor were
there novels about murder and scandal.

if the latter is written basically as their own. In a language, however, that spells *rough* so differently from *cuff,* and *though* so differently from *beau, cough* so differently from *off,* and *through* so differently from *true,** how can the transfer be made?

The discrepancies, in fact, of English spelling seem to be innumerable. There are over twenty ways of spelling the combination of sounds found in *shun.* The most common, of course, is *tion* as in *notion,* but *ssion* is pronounced the same way in *passion* as also is *tien* in *patient.* The puzzled tribesman in the Northwest Territory of Australia who wants to become literate in English has to have a good memory to recall when to spell *shun* with *tion* or *ssion* or *tien* or perchance with one of sixteen other combinations of letters. I, for one, would have to resort to the dictionary at least half of the sixteen times.

In the tribesman's tongue the sound $\overline{oo}$ of *boo* is probably written with *u* and in no other way. He must learn that in English, however, it is written in at least fifteen different ways: *oo, wo, ew, o, oe, ou, eu, ough, ue, u, ooh, ui, uh, oup,* and *ieu* as in *too, two, new, to, shoe, toucan, neuter, through, sue, duty, pooh, juice, Unruh, coup* and *lieu.* We have pointed out already that there are twenty-one ways in English to write one sound. It is the sound of the first person singular nominative pronoun, *I.* A few examples are: *eye, aye, igh* as in *sigh, ie* as in *tie, uy* as in *buy,* and *ia* as in *diamond.* How can the aborigine, who has learned that in his mother tongue *i* is always *ī,* transfer to reading English, his national language, with its countless variations in spelling? And if he does not learn to read and write the national language, how can he become a useful citizen of Australia? There is no other recourse. Full citizenship and progress are dependent upon his learning that

---

* rough-cuff   (ough=uff);   though-beau   (ough=eau);   cough-off (ough=off);   through-true   (ough=ue).

every vowel in the English language is pronounced five or more different ways.

For example, the letter *o* is pronounced differently in each of the following words: *no, do, or, doll, women, love, on, one.* What a relief to return to his own language in which *o* is always *o* as in *go* or *no*! If he knew that the people of Azerbaijan and of Daghestan had changed their alphabets twice in order to facilitate literacy and progress in general for their minority language goups, he would doubtless wish that someone would bring the spelling of English into a phonemic pattern.

If English were spelled phonemically it would be much more the world language than it is. India might not have discarded it for Hindi, nor the Philippines for Pilipino (Tagalog), nor New Guinea for Pidgin, when all of their scholars from hundreds of different language groups spoke it already. It might yet spread over three-fourths of Africa not just as the tongue of the scholars but as the second tongue of everyone who goes to school. Latin Americans would learn it with relative ease especially *if the new English alphabet conformed to the Spanish alphabet insofar as the latter is phonemic.* This would not be imperialism.

Some Filipinos, anti-imperialists, if you please, still favor English as a second language for everyone, even with its difficult system of spelling. They favor it "as a worldwide link language." A newspaper in Manila summarized their reasons for opposing the imposition of a local Philippine language on the other eighty or more language groups as follows:

1. *It will generate divisiveness among the people rather than forge unity among them. Regional differences will be sharpened, hence, this will create ethnic enclaves hostile to one another.*
2. *We will be cutting ourselves off from the world of culture, in fact from civilization. Every new idea and theory, each new truth that is discovered, is*

> *almost immediately translated in English if not ac-*
> *tually propounded in that language. Besides the*
> *tremendous outlay involved in translations, we do*
> *not have adequate skills to do the job.*
> 3. *Where internationalism is the order of the day, this*
> *proposal espouses the narrowest brand of national-*
> *ism. Instead of broadening our intellectual hori-*
> *zons, it proposes instead isolationism. An isolated*
> *outlook would reject anything foreign, however*
> *good.*

Philippine enthusiasts for "a worldwide link language" con-
sider their viewpoint even more patriotic than that of the
nationalists who insist on a strictly Philippine language as the
national tongue. That feeling is also found in other multilanguage areas. An Australian educator, W. C. Wentworth, Min-
ister-in-Charge of Aboriginal Affairs, a lifelong friend of New
Guinea who sincerely defends its interests, wrote me as follows
concerning New Guinea's seeming loss of a chance at having
"a worldwide link language" as its national tongue:

> *Fifteen years ago [1955] Pidgin was virtually un-*
> *known in the highlands and by no means universal in*
> *Papua where Police Motu still had some kind of hold.*
> *Today, however, Pidgin has almost become a national*
> *New Guinea language. I would fear that an attempt to*
> *oust it by proper English would not only cause resent-*
> *ment but would probably fail. I say this with great*
> *regret. . . . There is no technical or other literature*
> *available so that speakers of Pidgin come to a dead end*
> *intellectually and technically.*

Why did England and the U.S.A. reject George Bernard
Shaw's strong appeal to rectify an atrocious system of spelling?*
The negative arguments included both the cost and the trouble,
and it is perfectly true that both would be great. I submit,

---

* *Time* Magazine, March 4, 1957: "The saving," said Shaw, "would
pay for half a dozen wars, if we could find nothing better to spend it on"
(p. 71).

however, that the cost is far greater and the problems more rugged if we continue with the present system.

It has been found that in spite of a great school system on which the U.S.A. spends astronomical sums, millions of its citizens cannot read satisfactorily. Those who did learn to read lost on the average a year and a half in doing so, in contrast with children who learn to read a phonemically written language. In round figures, the present generation of Americans have lost 300 million student-years in learning to read. If they do much writing, most of them lose hours every year consulting dictionaries. Typists and printers have to strike 10 percent more keys and publishers have to use 8 percent more paper in printing books and periodicals than would be necessary with a phonemic alphabet.

Will the U.S.A. learn the lesson of the Caucasus regarding bilingual education and also the correction of the alphabet? Even though courage should fail short of alphabet reform, bilingual education, properly carried out, is a must for the sake of the "millions of children of limited English-speaking ability." The U.S.A. needs the contribution those youngsters would make to the nation's progress. Furthermore, if all of Latin America effectively followed a bilingual approach to the problem of educating its numerous exotic language groups, those groups, instead of serving as a handicap, would make a valuable contribution to progress.

The rest of the multilanguage areas of the world also urgently need to expand whatever attempts they may be making at erasing illiteracy and uniting their local language groups linguistically. It is important for all to open their eyes and learn. The problems so common to vast areas in the world can be solved. Let us review what is essential.

There must first be *concern*. The problem in the Caucasus, as has been noted, was diligently attacked almost from the start of the revolutionary regime. But who will show that kind of concern in the rest of the world and stick with it? Who will arouse people to action? Will it be educators, missionaries, enthusiastic linguists, political reformers, Utopian dreamers, or tough military leaders bent on rectifying a long-standing offense against minority groups?

A report, rendered to the Office of Indian Affairs in Washington on December 13, 1825, states:

> *The wise and the good have never ceased, from the earliest periods of our intercourse with the Aborigines of this country, to attempt, in one form or other, their rescue from barbarism, and to introduce among them the conveniences and the blessings of civilized life. But those kind designs were limited in their operations, and partial in their effects. . . . The most that was accomplished by the missionaries of those early and interesting periods, was to reform comparatively few Indians, and control in some degree, the savage ferocity of others; maintain and keep alive the spirit of kindness toward them, and to secure to themselves, as laborers in a cause so holy, an enviable immortality.*

During the nearly 150 years that have elapsed since that was written, the savagery amongst the Indians of the U.S.A. has of course disappeared. It went out with the fierce Apache warrior, Geronimo (1829-1909). Today the Apaches no longer carry rifles on the pummels of their saddles except when they join the army. Some of them carry instead a volume of Scriptures in Apache produced a few years ago by two linguists, Miss Faye Edgerton and Miss Faith Hill, working with Mr. Britton Goode of the Apache tribe. I heard a distinguished Sioux Indian, former U.S. Congressman Ben Reifel of South Dakota, tell a group that he was a member of Congress because of his mother's hymn book and Bible *in the Sioux language.* A missionary named Riggs had learned his language and translated the Scriptures a century earlier.

The great Dominican missionary of the sixteenth century,

Bartolomé de las Casas, emphasized the use of the local tongues in the areas of Mexico and Central America where he and his associates labored. John Eliot did the same in Massachusetts. He gave the Indians the complete New Testament in their own tongue, the tribe disappearing by integration, we are encouraged to believe, rather than by annihilation, as has happened in some cases both in North and South America due to disease, neglect, or "civilized savagery." Las Casas and Eliot, however, were exceptions. For the most part, missionaries did not learn the Indian tongues. Neither did government agents and educators. These spent vast sums of money in the U.S.A. maintaining schools for Indians on and off of the reservations, but the rate of illiteracy and monolingualism continued to be a problem. They were well meaning people, but they sought to impose English by substitution rather than win it a welcome by duplication. The results have left much to be desired.

Concern, then, whether it be the result of professional drive or religious brotherhood, is not enough. It must be followed by *proper methodology in action*. A literacy missionary, the late Frank Laubach, is credited with having assisted 100 million people on the path to literacy between 1920 and 1970, but he did not do it by just motivating them. He was expert at that, but he also expounded methods which speeded up results. His hands were tied, however, if the local languages weren't written. Right methodology, it is worth repeating, requires the use of the local languages, and in hundreds of places the local language has never been written. Hence, linguists must be trained and sent to all such language groups. Then teachers have to be prepared, and these should be native speakers of the language as well as apt speakers of the national tongue. Bilingual instruction must be introduced in the classroom at an early stage, certainly by the third or fourth grade. Reading materials in the local language as well as the national must be provided. Radio broadcasts, newspapers, plays, and religious services should be made available in the local tongue to pave the way for culture, recreation, and devotion in the national tongue. These must be amply financed. In the case of English and French the alphabet should be made phonemic.*

All the foregoing formed a part of the program in the Caucasus, including even the translation of the Bible into modern Armenian. The results, as we have seen, are an educated and united people where illiteracy and strife had prevailed. In fifty years horizons have been broadened and the path of progress opened. One main tongue, Russian, duplicates with dignity and new facilities the numerous local tongues that previously had stood alone, each with its very limited outlook.

In the rest of the world, at least 2,500 language groups have yet to be incorporated into the lifestream of their own nations where they live as foreigners.

At least 2,000 of the languages are unwritten. How can the speakers themselves reduce their languages to writing? I know of only one untrained tribesman who gave his people an alphabet. He was a Cherokee Indian named Guess, better known as Sequoyah. According to an article that appeared in the *Cherokee Pheonix*, August 13, 1828 (Vol. 1, No. 24), he spoke only his unwritten native Cherokee and consequently was illiterate. However, he invented an alphabet of eighty-six symbols and taught his neighbors to read their own tongue even though they could not read or understand English. The article goes on to say:

> *They succeeded in a few days, and from this it quickly*
> *spread all over the [Cherokee] nation, and the Cherokees*

* If this is not done, it would help, in giving the first bilingual instruction in reading, to use a special primer in which the national tongue is written phonemically with the same letters as are used in the local tongue plus or minus whatever symbols are lacking or in excess in the local tongue.

*(who as a people had always been illiterate) were in the
course of a few months, without school, or expense of
time, or money able to read and write in their own
language.*

That did happen once, incredible though it seems; but only
once. Two thousand more groups require phonemic alphabets
and they need them now. The alphabets must facilitate as much
as possible the transfer from the local to the national tongue.
Knowing myself the problems and frustrations that confront
such pioneer linguistic work, I estimate that 3,000 linguistic
teams are needed to reduce to writing and lay the groundwork
for the utilization in the classroom of 2,000 tongues. Many of
these teams of workers could come from the language groups
themselves if their governments saw to it that outstanding,
though necessarily in most cases, rustic individuals are selected
and given the training necessary. Dedicated linguists could be
brought in from the outside or, faster and better yet, both
outsiders and local workers could be used.

The Indonesian Government has contracted linguists of
the Summer Institute of Linguistics to help record its local
languages and simultaneously train Indonesians to participate
in and eventually lead in all that needs to be done for the
local groups. This type of cooperation will speed up the work
greatly. However, the 3,000 teams of linguists are needed
worldwide as soon as possible, and time is required to train
them. The most optimistic estimate would call for fifteen years
to get them all trained, located, and at work on 2,000 tongues.
Five more years are needed for an adequate analysis of the
languages, the preparation of teaching materials, the recruit-
ing of tribesmen willing to become teachers, and the stimulat-
ing of confidence and interest among all the groups. As soon
as possible would come the sending of gifted tribesmen off to
national centers of education, the bringing of them back, the
equipping of them, the scattering of them out among their

Hills and rugged terrain form the background for these schoolchildren in the Lezghian part of Daghestan.

people to start schools, and then the constant backing of them with financial support and encouragement. Where large groups are concerned, most of the other elements of the Caucasus educational approach should follow.

Will this be done? Is there motivation? If adequate motivation does not exist in religious circles to provide large numbers of las Casas, Eliots, and Laubachs; if there are not enough concerned educators; if governments are so much more preoccupied about further development of their progressive areas than about the splintered illiterate groups that they will not give sufficient funds, then there is not much hope for the 2,500 minority language groups. Nor is there much hope for the illiterate sectors of many nations. The thought is frightening. Perhaps that very fear will drive us to action.

It must be action. The alternatives are intolerable. The December 1971 issue of *Reader's Digest* presents one alternative.

It is found in an article by Lester Velie entitled "Give Us This Day Our Daily ABC's." After telling of progress in literacy being made through a special program in Kansas City among ghetto children, he quotes a warning from the Urban Coalition as follows: "Unless public education is changed, some nine million children, now enrolled in the public schools (of the U.S.A.) will enter the labor market as economic illiterates." Mr. Velie adds: "For want of their ABC's, they will be unable to earn their daily bread." Then they will fall into welfare rolls like their parents and grandparents before them. Apart from the successes attained by new methods in Kansas City during the past five years and more recently in Philadelphia, the article tells of costly failures. Nine billion dollars of federal funds were spent "on efforts to break the ghetto-school failure cycle" but to little avail.

With regard to isolated and primitive language groups, the relentless juggernaut of commercial progress rolls on. New oil fields with guns and diseases and roads of penetration bringing settlers and exploiters and soldiers are invading the forested, mountainous, or desert domains of the once isolated tribesmen. There is no escape apart from incorporation into society. This is practical on a large scale only through a vigorous bilingual drive. It should be worldwide.

Action is urgent! Divergencies between language groups of the U.S.A. as well as illiteracy can be routed. The Quechua-Spanish millions of the Andean highlands can be made happy participants of the national culture. The language groups of the Philippines, India, Nigeria, and other nations can be made to feel at home in the national tongue and be given the opportunity to excel that literacy and education provide.

It will not be by astronomical government grants for inadequate programs. It will not be through the policy of big foundations to give scholarships for higher education but nothing to help the 160 million illiterates who speak unwritten tongues. It will not be through churches that spend over two billion dollars annually in the U.S.A. on buildings but ignore the need of 2,500 minority groups imprisoned by their own exotic tongues. Nor will the anthropological protagonists of the "happy savage" theory usher in the better day they feel would rob the tribesmen of their own identity.

The solution will come as all of us who really want a united and harmonious society push for progress along the bilingual trail. Widespread concern plus the essentials of the Caucasus methods plus cooperation plus confidence plus continuity will bring success. The appalling plight of our fellow men who cannot understand their neighbor's speech nor read and write their own will then give way to a new day.

APPENDIX

Proposed New English Alphabet
Based on the Spanish Alphabet (Spanglish)

CORRELATIONS			DEVIATIONS		
SPANISH	NEW ENGLISH		SPANISH	NEW ENGLISH	
a	a	arm	ch	c	cik (cheek)
e	e	ple (play)	h (silent)	h	hom (home)
i	i	ski	j	j	jel (jail)
o	o	hom (home)			
u	u	yu (you)	ADDITIONS (sounds not occurring		
b	b	barn	in Spanish)		
c, k, qu	k	tek (take)		ạ	rạt (rat)
d	d	dans (dance)		ẹ	gẹt (get)
f	f	frut (fruit)		ị	wịl (will)
g	g	go		ọ	ofḷ (awful)
l	l	lek (lake)		ụ	ụp (up)
m	m	most		ū	pūt (put)
n	n	nem (name)		ṭ	iṭr (ether)
p	p	ple (play)		ḍ	iḍr (either)
r	r	rut (root)		ṣ	ṣi (she)
s	s	si (see)		ẓ	lẹẓn (leshon)
t	t	tut (toot)	(syllabic)	ḷ	apḷ (apple)
v	v	vot (vote)	"	ṇ	waitṇ (whiten)
w	w	wi (we)	"	ṛ	gṛl (girl)
x	x	fax (fox)			
z	z	zon (zone)			

(General American English based on pronunciation as found in *The Random House Dictionary*, 1967.)

We the peoples of the United
Nations determined to save suc-
ceeding generations from the
scourge of war, which twice in
our lifetime has brought untold
sorrow to mankind, and to reaf-
firm faith in fundamental human
rights, in the dignity and worth
of the human person, in the
equal rights of men and women
and of nations large and small,
and to establish conditions under
which justice and respect for the
obligations arising from treaties
and other sources of international
law can be maintained, and to
promote social progress and better standards of life in larger
freedom, and for these ends to
practice tolerance and live together in peace with one another
as good neighbors, and to unite
our strength to maintain international peace and security, and
to ensure, by the acceptance of
principles and the institution of
methods, that armed force shall
not be used, save in the common

Wi ḍi pip̦ls u̧v ḍi Yunaitiḍ
Nęṣu̧ns ditr̩mu̧nd tu sev su̧ksid-
ing jęnrȩṣu̧ns fru̧m ḍi skr̩ju̧s u̧v
wǫr wi̧c twais i̧n aur laiftaim hạz
brǫt u̧ntold saro tu mạnkaind,
ạnd tu rîufr̩m feţ i̧n fu̧ndu̧męntl̦
hyumu̧n raits, i̧n ḍi di̧gni̧ti ạnd
wr̩ţ u̧v ḍi hyu̧mu̧n pr̩su̧n, i̧n ḍi
ikwl̦ raits u̧v męn ạnd wi̧mu̧n ạnd
u̧v nęṣu̧ns larj ạnd smǫl, ạnd tu
ęstạbli̧ṣ ku̧ndi̧ṣu̧ns u̧ndr̩ wi̧c
ju̧stu̧s ạnd rispękt fǫr ḍi ạbli-
gęṣu̧ns u̧raizi̧ng fr̩u̧m tritis ạnd
u̧dr̩ sorsu̧s u̧v i̧ntr̩nạṣu̧nl̦ lọ ku̧n
bi mcntęnd, ạnd tu promot sọṣl̦
pragrȩṣ ạnd bȩţr̩ ṣtạndr̩dз u̧v
laif i̧n larjr̩ fridu̧m, ạnd fǫr ḍiz
ęnds tu pr̩ạktis tạli̧u̧ns ạnd li̧v
tugȩdr̩ i̧n pis wi̧d wu̧n u̧nu̧dr̩ ạz
gūd nebr̩s, ạnd tu yunait aur
strȩngt tu mentęn i̧ntr̩nạṣu̧nl̦ pis
ạnd sikyuri̧ti, ạnd tu i̧nṣur, bɑi
ḍi ạkзȩptu̧nз u̧v pri̧nзip̦lə ạnd ḍi
i̧nsti̧tuṣu̧n u̧v męłu̧ds, ḍạt armd
fǫrs ṣạl nat bi yuzd, sev i̧n ḍi
kamn̦ i̧ntri̧st ạnd tu ęmploi i̧n-
tr̩nạṣu̧nl̦ mu̧ṣi̧nri fǫr ḍi promọṣu̧n
u̧v ḍi ęku̧namik ạnd soṣu̧l ạd-

interest, and to employ international machinery for the promotion of the economic and social advancement of all peoples, have resolved to combine our efforts to accomplish these aims. Accordingly, our respective Governments, through representatives assembled in the city of San Francisco, who have exhibited their full powers found to be in good and due form, have agreed to the present Charter of the United Nations and do hereby establish an international organization to be known as the United Nations.

vạnsmụnt ụv ọl pipḷs, hạv rizalvd tu kụmbain aur ẹfṛts tu ụkampḷiṣ ḍiz ems. Ụkọrdịngli, aur rịspẹktịv Gụvṛnmẹnts, ṭru rẹprịzẹntụtịvs ụsẹmbḷd ịn ḍi sịti ụv Sạn Frạnsịsko, hu hạv ẹxịbịtụd ḍẹr fūl paurs faund tu bi ịn gūd ạnd du fọrm, hạv ụgrid tu ḍi prẹzṇt Çarṭṛ ụv ḍi Yunaitịd Nẹṣụns ạnd du hịrbai ẹstạbḷiṣ ạn intṛnạṣụṇḷ ọrgạnịzẹṣụn tu bi non ạz ḍi Yunaitịd Nẹṣụns.